It began to look as though the world would never know what the ancient Egyptians had to say about themselves.

Then came a hot summer day in 1822—just twelve months after Napoleon had died in lonely exile on the island of St. Helena.

All that morning a young Frenchman named Jean François Champollion had been working over a sheaf of hieroglyphs on his desk. As the clock struck noon, he rose unsteadily to his feet. Gathering up his papers, he rushed to a nearby library where his brother was working. Flinging his papers down on his brother's desk, Champollion cried: "*Je tiens l'affaire! Je tiens l'affaire!* [I've got it! I've got it!]"

And then he fainted dead away.

The Pharaohs of Ancient Egypt

By Elizabeth Payne

Landmark Books®
Random House New York

 Published in the United States by Random House Children's Books, a division of Random House, Inc., New York, and simultaneously in Canada by Random House of Canada Limited, Toronto. Originally published by Random House, Inc., in 1964.

www.randomhouse.com/kids

Cover art courtesy of Richard T. Nowitz/CORBIS. Reproduction of an ancient hieroglyph depicting the Pharaoh and his attendants at a harvest.

Library of Congress Cataloging-in-Publication Data
Payne, Elizabeth Ann. The pharaohs of ancient Egypt. (Landmark books)
SUMMARY: Discusses the life and history of ancient Egypt from the earliest times through the reign of Rameses II, as it has been pieced together from the work of archaeologists. 1. Pharaohs—Juvenile literature. 2. Egypt—Civilization—To 332 B.C.—Juvenile literature. [1. Egypt—Civilization—To 332 B.C. 2. Kings, queens, rulers, etc.] I. Title. [DT83.P3 1981] 932.01 80-21392 ISBN: 0-394-84699-0

Printed in the United States of America 48 47 46

Contents

The Pharaohs of Ancient Egypt

The Rediscovery of Ancient Egypt

A.D. 1798 to A.D. 1822

On a sweltering August morning in the year 1799, the Egyptian sun beat down on a scene of frenzied activity in the Nile River Delta. There, not far from a little town called Rosetta, a company of French soldiers was digging with a speed born of desperation. They were members of young Napoleon Bonaparte's Egyptian Expeditionary Force. And they were under threat of attack from both land and sea.

All morning their commanding officer, Major Pierre Bouchard, had forced himself to move cheerfully among his men. But now, his back to his troops, he was staring bleakly out at the Mediterranean Sea. It was useless to go on acting as if all were well. The French army faced disaster. Napoleon's Egyptian campaign, which had begun so brilliantly, was ending in catastrophe.

Just twelve months earlier, Napoleon had conquered Egypt in a lightning campaign of three weeks' time. From that moment on, everything had gone wrong. England, fearing that French control of Egypt would threaten her vital land and sea routes to India, had ordered her fleet to the Mediterranean. Shortly after Napoleon had entered Cairo in triumph, the British navy surprised the French fleet at anchor near Alexandria. In a fierce naval battle, the English blew up and sank most of Napoleon's ships, leaving Bonaparte and his forces stranded in Egypt.

Hard on the heels of this first calamity came a second. Egypt belonged to the Turks in 1798; it was part of their vast Ottoman Empire. Napoleon had assumed that the aged Turkish Empire was too enfeebled to fight his seizure of the Nile Valley. But Bonaparte was wrong. Not long after the British had destroyed the French fleet, the outraged sultan in Constantinople declared war on the upstart French general. Turkish troops and ships were dispatched southward to throw him out of Egypt.

And this was not all. Blockaded by the British and beset by the Turks, the stranded French faced still another enemy. Egypt's military aristocracy, the fierce Mameluke cavalrymen, refused to accept defeat. After their first rout by Napoleon, they had galloped off into the desert to regroup their forces. Now they were reported to be thundering back toward Cairo, bent on revenge. Faced with these three formidable foes, the desperate French were digging in wherever they found themselves.

"Major Bouchard!"

Behind Bouchard's back, a soldier had scrambled up over the top of his trench. There was a puzzled expression on his grimy, sweat-streaked face.

"Major Bouchard, sir!"

The call brought Bouchard back to the present. He turned, saw the beckoning soldier and made his way through the heat and dust and confusion to the man's side.

"Beg pardon, sir," the soldier said uncertainly. "It may be nothing, but would you have a look down there?"

Bouchard bent forward. In digging a trench, the soldier had uncovered the ruins of an old wall. Embedded among its crumbling yellow bricks—and winking up at Bouchard like a huge black diamond—was a chunk of polished stone. It was about two and a half feet across and three and a half feet high.

In spite of his troubles, Bouchard felt a flicker of interest. For the face of the stone seemed to be almost completely covered with a chiseled inscription. The Major jumped down into the trench for a closer look.

Squatting on his heels and narrowing his eyes against the sun's glare, Bouchard studied the stone with surprise. Its flat surface was divided into three sections. And each section was engraved with a block of writing in a different language.

Across the top of the stone were fourteen lines of what Bouchard recognized as hieroglyphs, the mysterious picture-writing used thousands of years ago by the ancient Egyptians. Directly below the hieroglyphs were thirty-two lines of a script Bouchard had never seen before. And crowded across the bottom of the stone were fifty-four lines of Greek.

Bouchard grunted and straightened up. The soldier

was watching him anxiously. "In view of General Bonaparte's order, sir," he said, "I thought . . ."

Bouchard cut him short with a nod of approval. Everyone in the expeditionary force knew of Napoleon's interest in ancient Egyptian history. Bonaparte had ordered his men to report at once any old curios or works of art they might come across in the course of their duties.

Well, Bouchard thought, the engraved chunk of stone was certainly ancient and undoubtedly a curio. But Napoleon was surely too hard-pressed at the moment to interest himself in an old fragment of black basalt. Still, an order was an order. With a shrug, Bouchard arranged to have the stone dug out of the ruined wall, and then reported the find to his superiors.

The black basalt was sent to Alexandria—and Bouchard forgot all about it. He had no idea that he and his soldier had made one of the most exciting archaeological discoveries of all time. For the Rosetta Stone, as the chunk of basalt came to be called, turned out to be the key to the lost history of ancient Egypt.

In Napoleon's day historians knew almost nothing about Egypt—past or present. It was a land the world had all but forgotten.

And yet once, long before the birth of Christ, Egypt had been the most famous and powerful country in the world. At a time in history when the ancestors of Western man still lived as semi-savages in the dense

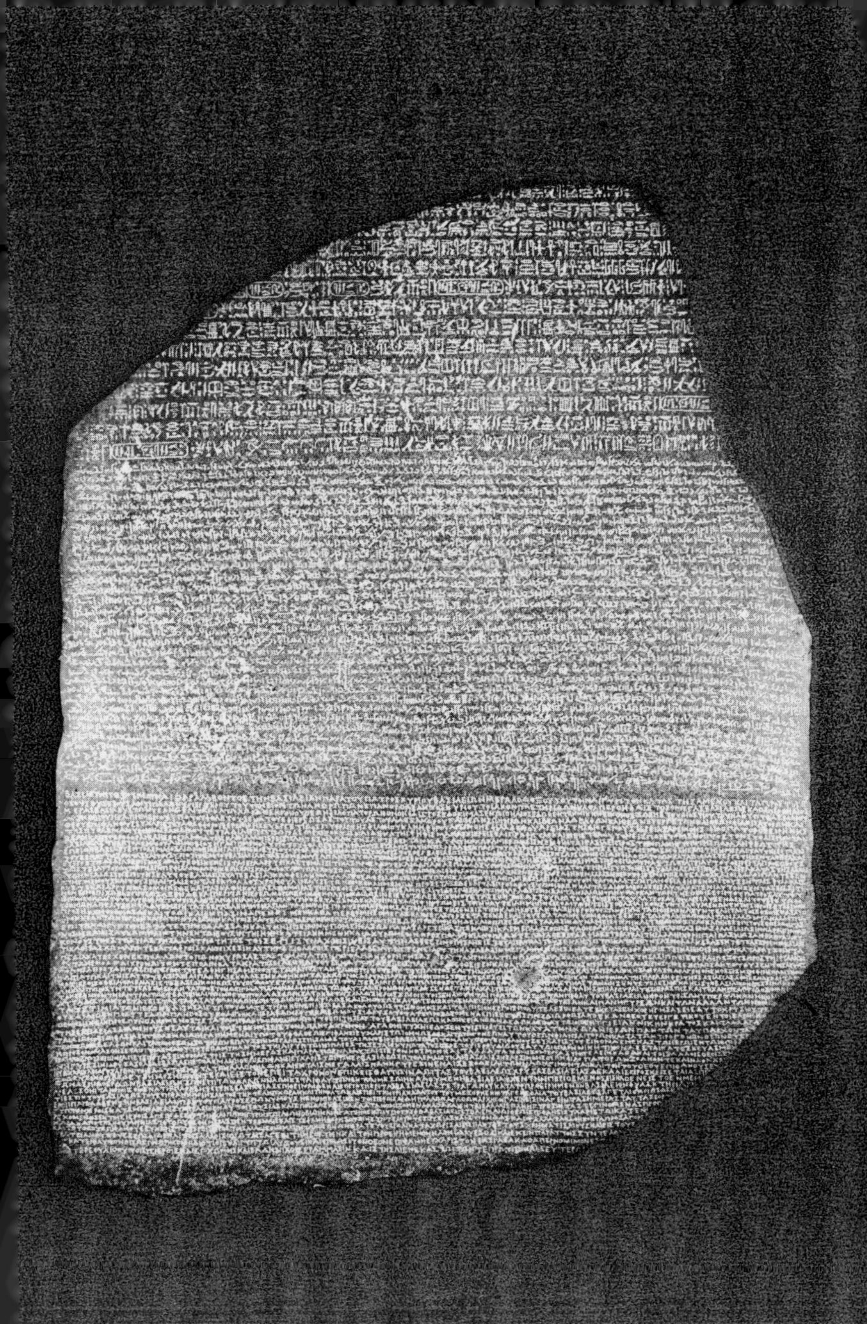

forests of England and Europe, a great civilization had existed along the banks of the river Nile. Ruled over by awesome god-kings called Pharaohs, Egypt had been a land of bustling cities, golden palaces, huge stone temples, busy dock sides and luxurious country estates. Her people had been fun-loving and light-hearted, her nobles elegant and worldly and her gods the most powerful in all the world.

This astonishing civilization had endured for more than 3,000 years, and then gradually vanished from the face of the earth. Its cities had crumbled to dust. The meaning of its writing had been lost. The story of its people, its Pharaohs and its days of greatness had been forgotten.

All that historians could say with certainty was that "once upon a time" a great and powerful people had lived in the Nile Valley. In proof of this there was the Bible, which told of the bondage of the children of Israel to the mighty Pharaohs of Egypt, thousands of years ago. And there were the accounts of Greek and Roman historians, such as Herodotus, who had visited and described ancient Egypt in the days of her decline. Above all, there was the testimony of the giant, half-ruined temples and pyramids that still stood along the banks of the sleepy Nile.

But the ruins, the Greek and Roman writers, and the Bible had nothing trustworthy to say about how ancient Egyptian civilization had come into being, or how it had developed. Historians in Napoleon's time knew almost nothing about the great Pharaohs. Nor did they know anything about the people who had lived in the Nile Valley so many thousands of years earlier. What had they and their god-kings been like? Whom had they worshiped? How had they lived out their daily lives? What had they thought of themselves and the world about them?

Napoleon wanted to know the answers to all these questions. So in addition to recruiting an army to invade the Nile Valley, he also persuaded more than 150 French scientists, artists and scholars to sail with him to Egypt. Many joined the expedition out of enthusiasm for Napoleon's plans to modernize Egypt. Others were inspired by Bonaparte's own intense curiosity about Egypt's ancient past. They signed on to investigate the ruined monuments along the Nile, and to gather material for a history of ancient Egypt.

This last was a bigger job than Napoleon and his scholars realized. For, as historians know today, there are only two reliable ways of learning anything about a long-vanished civilization. The first is by being able to read its language. The second is by scientific excavation of the often buried ruins of its villages and cities. And by the careful analysis of the artifacts, or objects of everyday use, found abandoned there—such artifacts as broken cooking pots and water containers, religious figurines, bits of jewelry and fragments of furniture.

But in Napoleon's day no one could read the writing of the ancient Egyptians: the secret of the hieroglyphs had been lost for 1,500 years. And archaeology, if it could be called that, had just been born.

Some years before Napoleon sailed for Egypt, an Italian peasant had uncovered an ancient wall when digging in his vineyard one day. The wall was part of the city of Pompeii, which had been buried under tons of hot ashes when Mount Vesuvius erupted in A.D. 79. In the years that followed, amateur enthusiasts—the world's first archaeologists—hacked their way down into the buried city. They excavated without plan or care, for today's painstaking archaeological techniques were, of course, unknown to them. As a result, they unwittingly destroyed almost as many priceless artifacts as they found.

But it was at Pompeii, nonetheless, that archaeology was born. It was to come of age in Egypt.

Once he had set up his own headquarters in captured Cairo, Napoleon established the Egyptian Institute as headquarters for his scholars. They were soon hard at work on their various projects.

Of them all, the French artist Dominique-Vivant Denon had the most exciting adventures in the months that followed. For when the defeated Egyptian cavalry galloped off into the desert to regroup its forces, Napoleon sent part of his army chasing after them. Denon went along as the representative of the Egyptian Institute.

As the French army followed its quarry deeper and deeper into Egypt, Denon began to have the eerie feeling that he was traveling straight into the past. He could

Ruins of an ancient Egyptian temple in Upper Egypt

scarcely believe the evidence of his own eyes. For the entire Nile Valley, hitherto almost totally unexplored by modern man, was like a great outdoor museum.

Each day's march up river along the Nile brought new wonders to light. Denon came upon huge, half-ruined stone temples, many buried almost to their rooftops in drifted sand. He saw slender obelisks, some rising like giant needles against the clear Egyptian sky, others lying broken on the ground. He stood beneath temple columns so big around that one hundred men could stand atop each one. He lifted his eyes in astonishment to the battered faces of statues seventy feet high. He crept down into musty tombs and gazed by flickering candlelight at wall paintings as vivid as the day they had been brushed on, 3,000 years before. And he stared with fascinated horror into the leathery, lifelike faces of ancient mummies, which were the embalmed bodies of men who had died thousands of years earlier.

All of these sights moved Denon "to a delirium of imagination." Time and again he nearly lost his life as he lagged behind the army to make drawings of the wonders he saw. When he returned to Cairo ten months later, his notebooks were bulging. In addition to detailed drawings of the ruins, Denon had also made careful copies of the many hieroglyphic inscriptions he had found on temple walls and obelisks.

Denon's colleagues at the Egyptian Institute examined his sketchbooks and listened to his report with astonishment. If they had needed proof that a mighty civilization had once existed along the Nile, here it was. But the ruins told only part of the story. The scholars knew by now that until they could read the mysterious hieroglyphs, the history of ancient Egypt would always remain a mystery.

A few days later—as if on cue—copies of the writing on the engraved chunk of black stone that Major Bouchard had found near Rosetta arrived at Institute headquarters.

They caused the liveliest excitement. For—from a description of the stone—two things were instantly clear to the scholars. First, the Rosetta Stone was part of a *stele*, a flat slab of stone on which the ancients used to engrave proclamations of importance. And second, this particular stele was trilingual. That is, the identical proclamation had been engraved on its face in three different languages.

Major Bouchard's superiors had recognized this and had realized its importance. For if all three languages on the stone said the same thing, and if any *one* of those three languages could be read, then the other two could probably be deciphered by transliteration. That is, letters and words in the known language could be matched up with letters and words in the unknown languages.

All of Napoleon's scholars could read Greek. In a matter of minutes, they had translated the fifty-four lines across the bottom of the stone. The words were a testimonial in praise of Pharaoh Ptolemy V for gifts he had given the Egyptian temples in 196 B.C.

The scholars' eyes flew to the hieroglyphs copied from the top of the stone. The meaning of the individual pictures was as mysterious as ever. But they now knew exactly what the whole block of hieroglyphic writing said. All that remained, they thought, was to match up each drawing to the known Greek letter below.

Napoleon was as excited as his scholars by this hope of at last deciphering the writing of the ancient Egyptians. In spite of his perilous military situation, he found time to have the writing on the Rosetta Stone copied and sent back to language experts in France.

Not long after this, Napoleon and most of his scholars were back in France themselves. The Egyptian campaign had proved a failure, and Bonaparte was urgently needed in Paris. Still later, the French army in Egypt came to terms with the British and the Turks, and the expeditionary force was brought home. The Rosetta Stone fell into English hands. Today it is one of the prize possessions of the British Museum in London.

During the next twenty years, as Napoleon's star rose and fell on the battlefields of Europe, scholars wracked their brains over the hieroglyphs on the Rosetta Stone. They had been able to decipher the unknown middle block of text without too much difficulty. The script was a modernized form of hieroglyphics called Demotic, which was written by the Egyptians of Pharaoh Ptolemy V's day.

But try as they might, scholars could make no sense of the hieroglyphs. The little pictures had no meaning at all when matched up to either the Demotic or Greek texts.

Wall paintings and sculpture adorn the walls of this eerie underground tomb.

"Hope has been abandoned of deciphering hieroglyphs," one language expert announced gloomily. And indeed, as scholars bogged down and fell to wrangling among themselves, it began to look as though the world would never know what the ancient Egyptians had to say about themselves.

Then came a hot summer day in 1822—just twelve months after Napoleon had died in lonely exile on the island of St. Helena.

All that morning a young Frenchman named Jean François Champollion had been working over a sheaf of hieroglyphs on his desk. As the clock struck noon, he rose unsteadily to his feet. Gathering up his papers, he rushed to a nearby library where his brother was working. Flinging his papers down on his brother's desk, Champollion cried: "*Je tiens l'affaire! Je tiens l'affaire!* [I've got it! I've got it!]"

And then he fainted dead away.

After years of painstaking labor, Jean François Champollion had at last deciphered the hieroglyphs. Not long before Champollion started to work, earlier scholars had made an important discovery. They had noticed that Pharaoh Ptolemy's name appeared five times in the Greek section at the bottom of the stone. And up in the hieroglyphic section there were five sets of identical picture signs, each encircled by an oval line. The scholars guessed that these encircled sets of hieroglyphs, which they called cartouches, spelled the name Ptolemy in ancient Egyptian. If this were so, they had learned the picture signs for seven letters of the alphabet.

It was a great step forward but, curiously enough, scholars failed to follow it through.

Champollion, however, began to collect copies of cartouches, which were now known to contain the names of ancient Egypt's kings and queens. In one cartouche that reached his desk, he recognized five of the same picture signs that appeared in Ptolemy's name. Leaving blank spaces for the unknown hieroglyphs, and filling in the signs he had recognized, Champollion's new cartouche read:

— L E O P — T — —

Champollion studied it for a moment, made a guess and then filled in the blank spaces. Now the cartouche spelled out:

K L E O P A T R A

If his guess was right (and it was), Champollion had learned the picture signs for three more letters of the alphabet. The Egyptians had no letter C.

Had intelligent guesswork like this been all there was to deciphering the hieroglyphs, the job would probably have been done long before Champollion's time. But when Champollion at last understood the grammar and syntax of ancient Egyptian writing, it was easy to see why earlier scholars had bogged down in despair.

For, as Champollion discovered, the Egyptian language contained an alphabet of twenty-four letter signs. But it did not form its words from letters alone, as modern languages do. Ancient Egyptian contained literally hundreds upon hundreds of additional hieroglyphs, some standing for sounds, some for concrete objects, some for abstract ideas. Champollion's genius somehow made order out of this seeming chaos. And not long after he fainted at his brother's feet on that summer day in 1822, he was able to give the world a tentative ancient Egyptian grammar and dictionary.

The excitement throughout educated Europe at the news of Champollion's feat can scarcely be imagined. Napoleon's scholars had by this time published thirty-six illustrated volumes of the wonders they had seen in the Nile Valley. The books had created the greatest enthusiasm. Americans and Europeans, whose knowledge of the ancient world had been limited almost entirely to Greece and Rome, were made dramatically aware that civilization had begun in Egypt and the Near East. Rich and highly developed cultures had once flourished there. Word that Champollion had deciphered the hieroglyphs gave hope that these cultures—or at least one of them—could be resurrected from the dead.

In the years that followed, all kinds of men flocked to Egypt. Some were sightseers, who voyaged up the Nile by excursion steamer to view the ancient monuments. Others were dealers and private collectors, on the lookout for ancient objects to buy and sell. Many were archaeologists.

Some of these archaeologists went to Egypt on their own; others were sent out by the great museums of Europe and America. They came prepared to dig up the past. For the great temples that Denon had drawn, drifted half over with sand, gave promise that other ancient marvels might lie buried beneath the desert.

Champollion had given archaeologists the ability to read the words of ancient Egypt's poets, storytellers, priests and Pharaohs. The archaeologists themselves were to write the rest of ancient Egyptian history with their spades. From Napoleon's day to this, their excavations in the Nile Valley have gradually brought to light the story of one of the world's first and greatest civilizations—the story of the people and Pharaohs of Ancient Egypt.

The First Egyptians and the Dead Demigods

From between 25,000 and 10,000 B.C. to 3200 B.C.

Some eighty or ninety years after Napoleon's campaign in Egypt, a group of archaeologists knelt one day around a shallow grave at the edge of the Egyptian desert. In the grave lay a skeleton, curled up on its side as though asleep. Beneath the body were the remains of a mat of woven rushes. And within reach of the hands were a few flint tools and some ancient clay pots.

The archaeologists stared silently down at the brittle brown bones. For a moment they forgot the hot Egyptian sun and the clouds of flies that danced in front of their eyes. For here, wonderfully preserved by Egypt's hot, dry climate, were the remains of a man who had lived in the Nile Valley some 7,000 years earlier.

Archaeologists were to find many of these ancient, primitive graves during their excavations in Egypt. The bones and artifacts they contained showed that the ancestors of the Pharaohs had been a small, slender people with dark, wavy hair. They had lived by hunting, and must have believed in some form of life after death. For they were buried with the tools and cooking pots they had used in this world and would presumably have need of in the next. These people were not the first inhabitants of the Nile Valley. But they were the first of whom any human trace had been found.

By this time archaeologists knew that the very first Egyptians of all had been forced into the valley by changes in the world's climate that took place sometime between 25,000 and 10,000 B.C. Before then, the Nile had not been a river at all. It had been a huge lake, or series of lakes. And the empty deserts that now stretch along the coast of North Africa had been covered with grassy plains and green jungles. On the other side of the Mediterranean Sea, most of Europe lay frozen beneath a great sheet of ice.

Then—no one knows for certain why—the world grew warmer and drier. Europe's ice cap began to thaw and recede. Rain stopped falling in the south, and the plains and jungles of the North African coast started to wither and die for lack of water.

As the drought intensified, the great Nile lakes began to shrink and dry up. In the end, nothing was left of them except a narrow river, about half a mile wide. It flowed to the sea at the bottom of the canyon it had once filled to the brim. This canyon—Egypt's famous Nile Valley—was about 750 miles long and from 12 to 31 miles wide. High limestone cliffs enclosed it on either side for most of its length. But about one hundred miles from the Mediterranean, these cliffs leveled off and the river divided into several channels. It then meandered down to the sea through a wide, fan-shaped tract of marshy lowland called the Delta.

Into this long, narrow canyon, to the banks of the river that was fast becoming their only source of water, moved the men and beasts of the dying North African plains. The valley must have seemed a watery paradise to them. The river teemed with fish. And the high reeds that choked its swampy banks were alive with wild ducks, wild geese and water birds of all kinds.

The great beasts which were the kings of this long-ago world entered the valley first. Thundering herds of giant bison, rhinoceroses and elephants led the way. Then came hundreds upon hundreds of the smaller animals —wild pigs and dogs, gazelles and donkeys, hyenas and goats.

And after the animals crept the men of that day. Driven by hunger and thirst, they made their way down into the valley by twos and threes or sometimes in loosely organized tribes. They lived on roots and small game, slept in treetops or caves and carried rough-hewn stone tools and weapons. They seemed scarcely more human than the wild animals they so feared.

Yet these same men, in the next several thousand years, took one of the most dramatic steps forward in the history of mankind. They became civilized.

In a world largely populated by near-savages, the Nile Valley men learned to plant seeds and grow crops. From

The Nile River at Aswan

wandering hunters who slept where the night found them, they became farmers living in settled villages. They learned to tame and use some of the least fearsome of the wild animals, such as donkeys and goats and oxen. They discovered metal, and were able to make copper instead of stone tools and weapons. They learned to cook and sew, to spin and weave, to sculpt and paint, to add and subtract. Most exciting of all, they learned how to read and write.

To archaeologists, it seemed almost a miracle that the Nile Valley men had learned to do all these things in such a short time. Several thousand years is a very short time indeed, compared to the hundreds of thousands of years that man had lived upon the earth in a state of almost complete savagery.

How and why had it happened?

Archaeologists cannot be absolutely sure. But their best guess is that the Nile River had a great deal to do with it. It behaved in a way that almost forced the Egyptians to use their wits if they were to survive, even as primitive farmers. And once man began to use his wits to control his environment, instead of letting his environment control him, civilization was not far behind.

The behavior of the river Nile has not changed in thousands of years. In ancient times, just as today, it went into full flood each year. Swollen by heavy seasonal rains at its sources deep in Africa, the river rolled north across the continent toward the Mediterranean Sea at twenty to thirty feet above its normal level. By the time it reached the upper borders of Egypt, most of its force had been spent. And so, instead of churning destructively down through the valley, it simply rose in a gentle swell and spread out over the valley floor. It covered the land for two to five or six miles on either side of its banks.

And there it stayed for four months, laden with the mud and silt it had gathered up on its long journey down into Egypt. When the flood waters at last receded and the river returned to normal, this mud and silt were left behind on the land. They made, and make today, one of the richest fertilizers in the world.

The ancient Pharaohs often called Egypt the Red Land and the Black Land, so startling was the contrast between the bands of black soil along the river banks and the reddish desert scrub that rose to the valley cliffs beyond.

The ancients also called the valley the Land of Kem. For *kemi* was the Egyptians' name for the river-borne silt on which their very lives as farmers came to depend. Without kemi there would be no Egypt at all. The Nile Valley would be as barren and unproductive as the deserts that surround it. This is what the ancient Greek historian Herodotus meant when he wrote that Egypt was "an acquired country, the gift of the river."

To the earliest Egyptians, however, the Nile's annual gift of kemi was more of a problem than a blessing. With luck, they could grow one quick crop after the flood waters receded. But more often than not, the rich black soil was of little use to them because there was almost no rainfall in Egypt. And without rain, the fertile kemi dried out and caked in a matter of weeks under the hot desert sun.

Faced with this problem, the prehistoric Egyptians first appealed to their gods for help. But prayer and sacrifice brought no more than an inch of rain (if that) each year. Next the valley men tried bringing river water to their fields in containers. This worked well enough for the little plots close to the Nile. But as farming increased, many plots were inland from the river. And so another solution had to be found.

"Who first?" is a question archaeologists often ask themselves as they study the distant past. Who first among the valley men, they wonder, realized that Egypt's lack of rainfall was of little importance—*if* the Nile waters could be trapped at flood time and stored in canals between the fields, ready to use on the crops when needed? Who first thought up what is known today as irrigation?

No one knows. All archaeologists can say is that sometime in the shadowy past the prehistoric Egyptians learned how to irrigate their fields. And from that time on, life began to quicken in the valley. Irrigation seemed to start a chain reaction by which one civilizing force led to another.

Before irrigation, for instance, the descendants of the first Egyptians had banded together in small villages along the river banks. There each man did everything for himself. He made his own tools and cooking pots. He built his own hut from river mud and reeds. He hunted his own game, fished for his own supper and haphazardly tried to grow a little wheat or flax on his patch of kemi.

Irrigation gradually changed all this. For it meant not only bigger and better crops; it also meant that two and sometimes three crops could be grown each year. Much more food was available. As a result, for the first time in their history, the prehistoric Egyptians knew some release from their relentless, age-old daily struggle to find enough to eat.

This new freedom gave the valley men time to look about them a little. With pleasure and surprise, they realized that a duck in flight was beautiful, as well as stomach-filling. And a silver fish, darting among the reeds at the river bank, was exciting to watch, as well as good to eat. Crudely at first, they began drawing the duck and the fish on the sides of their pottery bowls. Then, little by little, over the long years their skill as artists increased and their everyday objects became as beautiful as they were useful.

With their new-found freedom, the valley men also began to specialize. Each man, instead of doing everything for himself, gradually began to do what he liked best, or was best able to do. Some villagers were natural-born farmers; they liked to work in the fields. Soon they began doing so all day. Others had a talent for engineering; they kept the irrigation ditches in order and busied themselves draining the swampy river banks to make more fields. Still others became expert at making tools, or in building light-weight river skiffs from papyrus reeds. Others were born hunters, skilled at netting water birds or finding the best fishing holes in the river or

The valley people began to decorate their pottery with animals and human beings . . .

to carve figures out of ivory tusks . . .

and to model animals in clay.

knowing just where game hid out in the desert behind the valley cliffs.

Each of these new specialists had to exchange his product or service for the other things he needed to live. The tool maker bartered a chisel for two cooking pots. Or the field worker exchanged a sheaf of wheat for a catch of fresh fish.

And so little by little over the long years a hustle bustle of trade began in the valley—both within the villages, and among the neighboring settlements strung out along the river.

Political changes followed. Groups of villages banded together under the strongest leader among them. These village groups expanded into provinces, and then into small kingdoms. By the year 3200 B.C., or thereabouts, the valley was divided into three such kingdoms, each ruled over by a powerful, prehistoric king.

The first kingdom was in the Delta of Lower Egypt. Here ruled the Bee King, whose official emblem was a bee, or hornet. The Bee King wore a red crown and ruled from a primitive palace called the Red House.

The second kingdom was in Middle Egypt, near present-day Cairo. This was the domain of the Reed King, whose symbol was the papyrus plant. He wore a high white crown and his palace was called the White House.

The third kingdom was in Upper Egypt near the First Cataract, a rocky rapids in the Nile that separated Egypt from her southern neighbors, the Nubians. This part of the valley was ruled over by the Hawk King, whose standard was copied from the falcons that soared high in the cloudless Egyptian sky.

Shortly before the year 3200 B.C., it is said that the Hawk Kingdom was governed by a mighty warrior called the Scorpion. Marching north, the Scorpion conquered the Reed King of Middle Egypt. His successor, who was now king of both Middle and Upper Egypt, went on to conquer the Delta kingdom of the Bee King. For the first time in its long history, the Nile Valley was united under a single ruler.

His name was Menes, and he was the first Pharaoh of ancient Egypt. With Menes, Egyptian history officially begins.

Nearly 3,000 years later, an Egyptian priest named Manetho wrote a history of his country. He referred to the Scorpion, the Reed, the Bee, and the Hawk kings as the Dead Demigods. Like all Egyptians, Manetho believed that his country's kings were half-mortal, half-god. And he believed that the Scorpion and his predecessors were the first of those half-mortal, half-divine Pharaohs who stepped out onto the stage of ancient history.

Manetho also divided the many Pharaohs of Egypt into thirty-one dynasties, or rulers of the same family. "After the Dead Demigods," he wrote, "the First Dynasty consisted of eight kings, of whom the first was Menes the Thinite; he reigned for sixty-two years and perished from the wound of a hippopotamus."

Historians cannot be sure that Manetho's dynastic divisions were accurate. But they have continued to use them as a matter of convenience.

Narmer, another name for Pharaoh Menes, is shown on this slate tablet or palette subduing the people of Lower Egypt. The King wears the high white crown of Upper Egypt and a kilt with a lion's tail attached at the back.

When Egypt was ruled by Pharaoh Menes, the valley people were divided into roughly two classes—rich and poor. The vast majority of Egyptians were (and would remain all through their history) tillers of the soil, simple peasants and serfs. Slightly above them in the social scale were the skilled craftsmen, a group that was to grow over the years. And at the top, just beneath all-powerful Pharaoh, was the nobility. This was a small, privileged class, made up of Pharaoh's relatives and the descendants of the prehistoric chieftains and kings.

The newly unified Egyptians had not changed much in appearance from their remote ancestors, the first men who came down into the valley. They were a little taller perhaps, averaging about five feet six inches in height. But they were as slender and slim-hipped as the valley men of 3,000 years before, with dark hair and reddish-brown skin. Though their thinking and way of life had changed much over the long, long centuries, they had retained their ancestors' belief in a life after death.

By Menes' time, however, the next world was no longer the hunter's paradise dreamed of by the early valley men. To the new Egyptians, the world beyond was just like the valley. And life would go on there much as it had on earth—provided certain precautions were taken.

No one, first of all, could enter this next world unless his earthly body was preserved from decay after death. Everything depended on this. If a man's body was allowed to disintegrate, his spirit, or *ka*, would be condemned to wander the deserts as a lonely ghost for all eternity. Believing this, the Egyptians became expert embalmers very early in their history. They immersed their dead for seventy days in special salt baths. Then they wrapped the body in yards and yards of resin-soaked strips of linen, inserting pads here and there to make the body look as lifelike as possible. The body was then supposed to endure forever—and so skilled were these embalmers of ancient Egypt that many mummies have, indeed, endured for thousands of years.

An ancient Egyptian priest had this portrait of himself carved on a wooden door in his tomb. He believed that the loaves of bread on the stand would magically turn into real bread in the next world.

If they were to live on in the next world as they had in this, the dead would have need of their earthly possessions. And so the poor were buried with their few cooking pots and tools, like the first valley men. And the nobles were laid to rest in tombs that contained rooms full of furniture and chests of clothing, food and ornaments. To make doubly sure that they would be surrounded in the hereafter with all the comforts they had enjoyed on earth, the nobles also covered the walls of their tombs with painted scenes from their daily lives. These vivid little pictures showed the noble dining with his family and friends, visiting his fields and vineyards, inspecting his herds and conferring with the overseer of his estate. They showed him boating on the Nile with his children, netting wild birds at the riverside with his wife and fondling his favorite hunting dog. Magic, it was believed, would bring these scenes to life again in the next world. And thus the noble would live on eternally, surrounded by the people and possessions that had been dear to him on earth.

At this time in Egyptian history, only Pharaoh could be absolutely sure of immortality. As a god, he would rejoin his fellow gods in the heavens after the death of his mortal body (while another god-king was sent to take his place on earth). But Pharaoh would need the services in afterlife of those who had served him on earth—his field workers, house servants, officials and nobles. And herein lay the hope of immortality for the Egyptian people themselves. For in these early days, all of Egypt—its land, its people, its vineyards, its livestock—was considered to be Pharaoh's private property. And so everyone could be said to serve Pharaoh in one way or another, whether or not he actually ever came into personal contact with this august personage. Thus the valley people could hope to enter the next world because their great god-king himself could not live on eternally there without them.

The unification of Egypt under Pharaoh Menes was followed by four hundred years of experimentation in the Nile Valley. It was a time when the valley men tried out all sorts of new ideas and ways of doing things. By the end of the four-hundred-year period they had worked out a way of life for themselves—and a set of beliefs about the world they lived in—that was to remain almost unchanged for the next 3,000 years.

They came to believe, first of all, that they were the chosen people of the ancient world. All through their history they were to describe foreigners as "vile" and "wretched."

They also believed that the great gods had created the sun-filled Nile Valley especially for them, placing it between two vast deserts in order to protect the Egyptians from the wandering and often warlike peoples of the Mediterranean world. And, as a special mark of favor, the gods had sent one of their own fraternity down into the valley to rule as king. This god in mortal form was Pharaoh.

There were many reasons why the ancient Egyptians needed to believe that their ruler was a god. The valley men lived in a pre-scientific world that knew nothing of natural causes. A flash of lightning, good or bad crops, birth and death, storms or drought—all these, they believed, were caused by unseen and all-powerful gods, gods who were angry, fearsome, vengeful, kind or cruel as the spirit moved them.

What better insurance against the unpredictable behavior of these awesome beings than to believe that

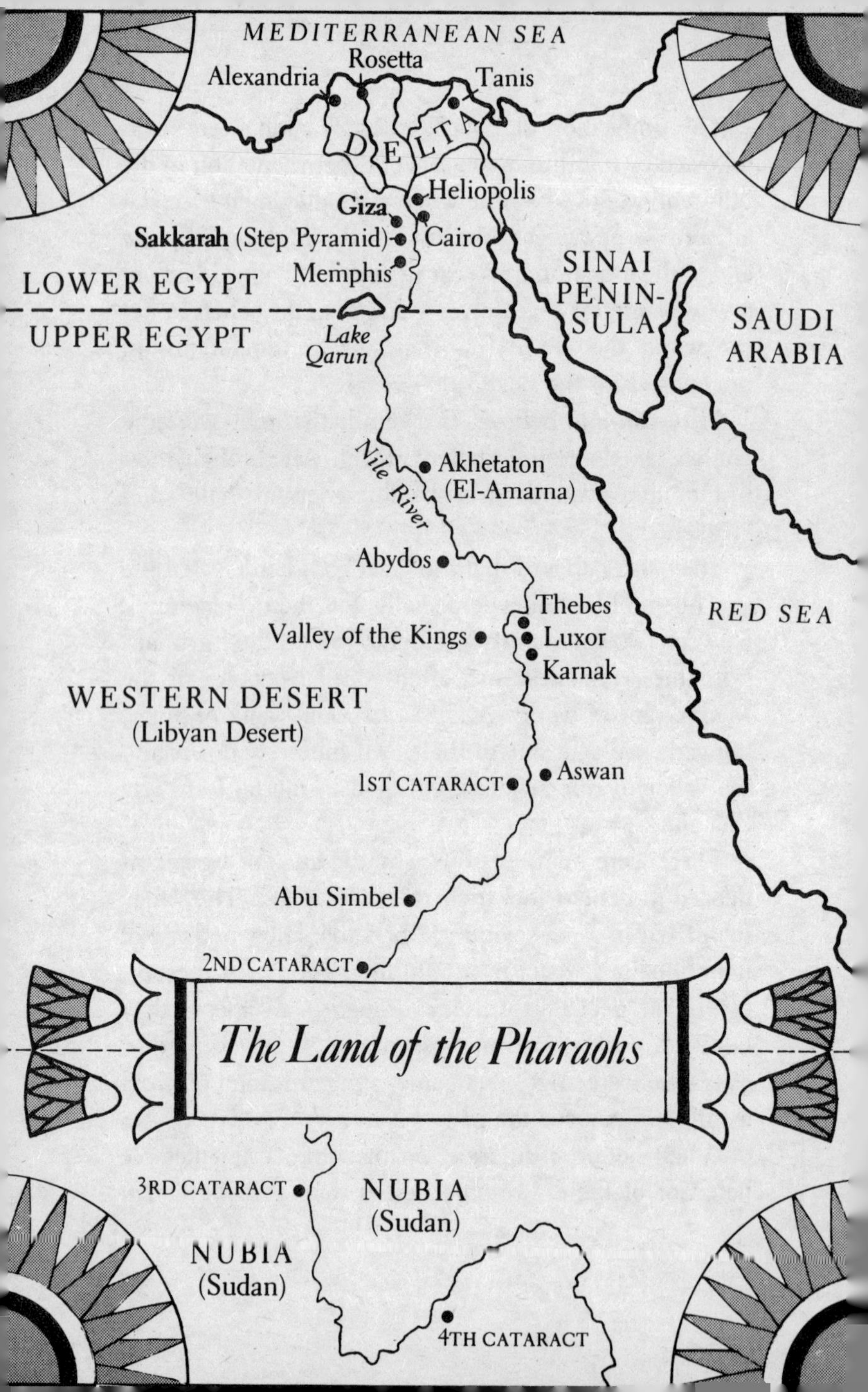
MEDITERRANEAN SEA
Rosetta
Alexandria
Tanis
DELTA
Heliopolis
Giza
Sakkarah (Step Pyramid)
Cairo
Memphis
SINAI PENINSULA
LOWER EGYPT
UPPER EGYPT
Lake Qarun
SAUDI ARABIA
Nile River
Akhetaton (El-Amarna)
Abydos
Thebes
Luxor
Karnak
Valley of the Kings
RED SEA
WESTERN DESERT (Libyan Desert)
Aswan
1ST CATARACT
Abu Simbel
2ND CATARACT
The Land of the Pharaohs
3RD CATARACT
NUBIA (Sudan)
NUBIA (Sudan)
4TH CATARACT

one of them sat on the throne of Egypt? Such a god-king would have Egypt's interest at heart. By reason of his extraordinary powers, he would insure that all went well in the valley, and that his brother gods acted in Egypt's favor.

The ancient Egyptians, for example, never knew that seasonal rains at the Nile's source caused the river to rise each year. They thought the Nile flooded on orders from the gods. If the gods were angry, they might refuse to send a good flood—or any flood at all. Then crops would die and famine cripple the land. As flood time approached each year, the entire valley grew increasingly uneasy and anxious.

"Strong and weak unite to beg thee . . . to grant thy waters," they prayed to Hapi, god of the Nile. "No man dons his raiment. The children of the great are not arrayed in finery, and songs are no more heard in the night."

A king who was a god could intercede with his brother god Hapi to make sure that the valley received a good flood each year. And this, in fact, became one of Pharaoh's most important duties. Every June, when the flood was due, he voyaged to Egypt's upper borders, where the waters first began to rise. There, in solemn ceremony, Pharaoh "spoke" to his brother Hapi and exacted his promise to send the kemi-laden waters down into the valley once again.

There also may have been a down-to-earth political reason behind the Egyptians' belief that their king was a god. Though the valley was now unified, the people of

Upper and Lower Egypt lived together much of the time in a state of misunderstanding and mutual rivalry. The two regions spoke entirely different dialects: a Delta man could barely understand the speech of the provincials in Upper Egypt. And the men of the Delta, in contact with the Mediterranean world beyond their shores, felt themselves to be more advanced and worldly than their country cousins up river. In spite of unification and the great river they shared in common, Upper and Lower Egypt tended to split into separate kingdoms again at the first sign of trouble.

A mortal king from either region would have intensified this rivalry. But a king who was a god stood above the battle, no matter where in the valley his human body had been born. As a god, therefore, Pharaoh acted as a strong unifying force, holding his country together as one nation, from Aswan to the Delta.

Even so, Pharaoh found it politically wise to acknowledge the differences and rights of the two regions. His official crown was a combination of the Red Crown of Lower Egypt and the White Crown of Upper Egypt. His palace was always built with two gates, the Gate of the North and the Gate of the South. And Pharaoh was never referred to as the King of Egypt. He was always called the Lord of the Two Lands, or the King of Upper and Lower Egypt.

In the four hundred years that followed the death of "Menes the Unifier," the Egyptians' belief in the divinity of their Pharaoh became so profound that they flung themselves face down in the dust at his approach. Too awesome to be mentioned by name, he was called the One, or the One Who Lives in the Great House—hence Pharaoh. For *Per-o* was the Egyptian word for Great House.

Pharaoh's heralds preceded him with the cry: "Earth, beware! Your god comes!" And a tale is told that certain death awaited any man who happened to touch this great and awesome person by mistake.

Such had Pharaoh become in the eyes of his people when one of the greatest of the early god-kings—Khufu or Cheops—ascended the throne sometime around 2756 B.C.

"The Good God"—Pharaoh Cheops

From about 2756 B.C. to about 2553 B.C.

About 450 years before Christ was born, the Greek historian Herodotus paid a lengthy visit to the land of Egypt. He stayed for a time in Memphis, the ancient capital of the Pharaohs. And while there, he went with a group of Egyptian priests to view one of the Seven Wonders of the World—the Great Pyramid of Giza.

The pyramid rose hugely from the flat desert near Memphis, a perfectly proportioned mountain of stone as high as a modern forty-story skyscraper. South of it, a line of smaller pyramids stretched for more than sixty miles along the banks of the Nile. Like Giza, each was the tomb of an ancient Egyptian Pharaoh or his Queen.

Herodotus stood bareheaded and mute beneath Giza's towering sides. Nothing in all his travels had prepared him for such a sight. More than two million blocks of granite, each averaging about two and a half tons in weight, had gone into the making of this giant structure. Its sides were covered with polished limestone as smooth

The giant sphinx at Giza

as glass. And at its peak a golden capstone flashed and gleamed like a beacon in the bright sunlight.

Giza, the priests told Herodotus, had been the tomb of Pharaoh Cheops, who had ruled Egypt more than 2,000 years earlier. Deep within the body of the pyramid, a series of secret passageways led to the King's Chamber. There stood the red granite sarcophagus, or stone coffin, that contained Cheops' mummy. Around it were grouped riches beyond imagining—caskets of jewels, ebony furniture inlaid with ivory and gold, silver and alabaster bowls and vessels, chests of clothing and precious ornaments, and jars of food and wine. For Cheops would have need of these things in the next world, just as he had needed them in this.

Standing in the triangular-shaped shadow cast by the huge stone tomb, the priests told Herodotus how the pyramid had been built. Herodotus wrote down everything they said. And what he wrote was read and believed for centuries to come.

Alexander the Great, Julius Caesar and Napoleon Bonaparte all read the works of the Greek historian. And each in turn, as he stood in awe beneath the Great Pyramid, imagined he could hear the groans of the slaves who had labored under the lash of Cheops' brutal overseers to raise this mighty tomb skyward.

For the priests had told Herodotus that when Cheops succeeded to the throne he "plunged into all manner of wickedness. He closed the temples and forbade the Egyptians to offer sacrifice, compelling them instead to labor, one and all, in his service."

The Great Pyramids of Giza, showing Cheops' tomb in the foreground with Chephren's tomb just behind it

Cheops, the priests went on, commandeered the people of the Nile Valley to build his pyramid for him. He ground them down "to the lowest point of misery. . . . One hundred thousand men labored constantly, and were relieved every three months by a fresh lot. It took ten years' oppression of the people to make the causeway for the conveyance of the stones. . . . The pyramid itself was twenty years in building."

Cheops' successor had been just as wicked as he, the priests told Herodotus. In fact, "The Egyptians so detest the memory of these kings that they do not much like even to mention their names."

Well, Egyptologists are not so sure about all this.

When American and European archaeologists first started to work in Egypt, around the beginning of the last century, they went directly to the Great Pyramid, both as sightseers and researchers. The huge tomb was some 4,500 years old by then. Its golden pinnacle had long since vanished. And its outer casing of polished limestone had fallen away, or had been carted off by the Arabs for building elsewhere.

The Arabs, too—or so it was supposed—had found the secret, blocked-up entrance to the tomb. For it was standing open. And when archaeologists crawled along the eerie inner passageways to the heart of the pyramid, they found the King's Chamber had been robbed. The furniture, jewels and clothing that could have told them so much about Cheops and his times had vanished. More disappointing still, the great red sarcophagus stood empty. Cheops' mummy had disappeared.

Like all students of the past, these pioneer archaeologists, too, had read and believed the accounts of Herodotus. But their excavations turned up no evidence that Cheops had been the heartless monster described by the Greek historian. On the contrary, all their findings —meager though they were for this early period— seemed to indicate that Cheops was a "Good God," whose people labored willingly, as an act of worship, to build a tomb worthy of his greatness.

Pharaoh Cheops ruled Egypt from the city of Memphis, which stood at the juncture of Upper and Lower Egypt, about ten miles up river from present-day Cairo. The city had been founded by Menes some 450 years earlier, to serve as the capital of his newly unified land.

Nothing remains today of this once bustling and beautiful metropolis. The ancient Egyptians built their tombs and temples of enduring stone. But their houses and the greater part of their cities were constructed of perishable brick. Little remains of them except dust heaps and an occasional crumbling wall.

Nonetheless, it is reasonable to suppose that Memphis was much like later Egyptian cities, about which more is known. In slow-to-change Egypt, which built very nearly the same kinds of houses, boats and temples for more than 3,000 years, it is unlikely that early cities differed radically from those built later on. If this is so, it is safe to give a description of what Pharaoh Cheops' thriving capital must have been like.

Memphis stood on the banks of the slow-moving Nile. Stone docks lined its busy waterfront, which was noisy from sunup to sunset with the coming and going of river traffic. Little fishing skiffs, carrying harpoons to ward off the river's fearsome crocodiles and hippopotamuses, skittered about beneath the bows of larger craft. Vegetable barges from the Delta maneuvered clumsily into

Model of a fishing and fowling skiff found in an Egyptian tomb. The man with the harpoon is poised to spear a Nile River catfish, or to frighten off an attacking hippopotamus.

port. Some carried peas, lettuce and watermelons for the tables of Pharaoh and his nobles; others brought garlic, radishes and onions for the Memphis poor. Seagoing ships lay at anchor, their holds laden with cedar wood from distant Lebanon on the eastern Mediterranean coast. For Egypt was rich in every natural resource except building timber, which she had to import. Smaller craft waited their turn to unload the ivory, ebony, ostrich feathers and gold dust they had brought down river from Nubia, Egypt's neighbor to the south. On the docks, stevedores sweated and overseers shouted as bellowing livestock and bales of grain were unloaded from barges that had come down river from Upper Egypt.

Beyond the cargo boats, the graceful river craft of the nobility rode at anchor. And in a slip of her own lay Pharaoh's Great Royal Barge, her oars shipped and her square red sail furled. (Prevailing winds enabled the Egyptians to sail up river; coming down river, they had to row.) At the very end of the dock side stood the shipyard, noisy with the sound of hammers, saws and shouted orders. For this was one of the busiest places in a land whose main highway was its river.

Narrow, twisting alleys led back from the docks into a crowded rabbit warren of taverns, mud-brick huts and workshops. Here lived the Memphis poor—her unskilled workers, dock hands, gold and copper smiths, weavers, potters and cabinet makers. They lived in squalid huts, furnished with a stool or two and perhaps a wooden bed. The men wore short kilts, and the women coarse linen shifts. The children ran about naked, and everyone went barefoot.

These people worked from sunup to sunset, the unskilled at backbreaking physical labor and the skilled at making delicate jewelry, fine linen, inlaid furniture and exquisite pottery for Pharaoh and his nobles. But despite their long hours of work and their lack of creature comforts, the poor of Memphis (and of all Egypt) seem to have been a merry lot. The valley was warm and sunny. The river teemed with fish. And as far as archaeologists can tell, the poor had few complaints. They went about their business cheerfully, relished their diet of fried fish, garlic and coarse bread and enjoyed the good strong beer of Egypt whenever they had the chance.

Beyond the dock-side quarters of the poor, the alleys widened out into the shady, tree-lined streets of the city's upper-class residential section. Here lived Pharaoh's nobles and the high-born officials who served him up and down the valley. Their houses were enclosed by high brick walls. And each had its own pool and garden, where pet gazelles picked their dainty way among the flower beds, and brightly colored birds sang in the acacia and sycamore trees.

The lords and ladies of these elegant dwellings lived their lives in service to Pharaoh. Each morning they breakfasted on fruit and light wine and then dressed themselves with care. The men wore heavy, biblike necklaces of gold and precious stones, and linen kilts, buckled around the waist with a jeweled clasp. On their heads they placed thick black wigs, and on state occasions they wore thonged sandals. Otherwise they went barefoot.

The women's preparations for the day were more elaborate. They painted a green line below their eyes, darkened the lids with black make-up, rouged their lips and stained their finger and toe nails red. Their clothing consisted of an almost transparent linen sheath and nothing else. They, too, wore long black wigs, and necklaces, bracelets and anklets of gold and jewels.

Archaeologists think the ancient Egyptians first wore

wigs to shield their heads from the valley's hot sun, and that eye paint was used as a protection against the sun's glare. But whatever their origin, wigs and eye make-up had become high fashion by Cheops' day.

The Royal Precinct where Pharaoh's lords and ladies spent their days was almost a city within a city. Just inside the gates of its high, encircling walls stood the Great Royal Storehouses. These were a noisy complex of cattle yards, granaries and warehouses, full to overflowing with the taxes paid to Pharaoh each year by his people. Coined money was unknown in ancient Egypt and tax payments were made in flax, wine, honey, grain, beer and livestock.

Close by the storehouses was the Great Royal Treasury. Here an army of scribes worked busily all year round. These men were a vital part of Egyptian society, and their importance was to increase as valley life and government became more complex over the years. Scribes were graduates of the temple schools, where they had learned to read and write. Some went on to serve the public. For a catch of fish or a length of linen, they would write a letter or record a business transaction for a client. Others worked in the households or on the vast country estates of the nobles, keeping their accounts and records. Some became teachers, and many hundreds worked in Pharaoh's employ. Those in the Great Royal Treasury spent most of their time bent over Pharaoh's tax lists. They kept track of taxes due, wrote out receipts for taxes paid and checked incoming payments of produce and livestock through to the storehouses.

The superintendent of an ancient Pharaoh's Royal Granary, with his wife and child

A royal scribe, his papyrus scroll open on his lap

A brewer straining mash

Beyond the bustling commercial section of the Royal Precinct was the quiet temple area, where Pharaoh worshiped daily. Many of Egypt's gods had temples there—but not all. For the valley people worshiped hundreds of deities. They ranged from obscure little village gods to the great creators of the world. There were gods of the sun and moon, of good and evil, of hearth and home, of wisdom and love, of death and resurrection—gods of all sorts and kinds. They personified everything the Egyptians wondered about or feared or hoped for. Reigning supreme over this multitude was Ra, the great god of the sun.

Bright banners fluttered from the flagpoles that stood before each of the precinct temples. Within, priests moved gravely about their duties. A privileged few busied themselves in the most sacred part of each temple—its inner sanctuary or holy of holies. Here was kept the image of the temple god, sometimes a golden statuette, more often a painted wooden figure with movable arms and legs. Each day the priests bathed and anointed these images. Then they changed the god's clothing and placed before him offerings of meat, fruit and cakes. (Magic, it was believed, would enable the god to absorb the essence of the food.)

Not far from the temples was a parklike area of shade trees, ornamental pools and brilliant gardens. Here were the palaces of the royal family. All were light, airy buildings, suitable to Egypt's hot, dry climate. The palaces were furnished simply, but richly, with gauzy linen hangings and chairs, tables, and couches made of precious woods, inlaid with gold or ivory. Nearby were the palace cookhouses, where the royal chefs worked over their roasting pits and brick ovens, preparing the roast duck, roast beef, grilled gazelle steaks and sweet cakes that graced Pharaoh's table.

Cheops conducted most of his governmental business from his imposing, pillared Audience Hall in the Royal Precinct—ably assisted by his nobles, his officials and his vizier or prime minister. But once a year he boarded his Great Royal Barge to make an inspection tour of the kingdom.

Sailing north, and then south, from Memphis, Pharaoh voyaged majestically from the Delta to the borders of Egypt. He noted the condition of the country's irrigation systems. He visited existing temples and commissioned his architects to draw up plans for building new ones. And he paid a state visit to the twenty or more provinces into which his land was divided. Each of these provinces had a name—the Province of the Jackal, the Double Scepter, and the Point of the Two Fishes, for example. And each was governed by one of Pharaoh's nobles, known as the First Under the King. It was the responsibility of these nobles to administer justice in their localities, to oversee the fields and the livestock, to maintain the area temples, to repair and enlarge their irrigation systems. They also collected the taxes due Pharaoh each year from their districts, and shipped them on to the Great Royal Treasury.

His inspection tour done, Cheops almost certainly made one more port of call before returning to his capital. Ten miles down river from Memphis, he would have dropped anchor for a day or two to see how work was progressing on the giant tomb he was building for himself—the tomb known today as the Great Pyramid of Giza.

The Egyptians first started to build with stone about one hundred years before Cheops was born. Before then, their buildings had been constructed of wood and of bricks made from Nile mud. When first used, stone was laid as flooring in a few occasional tombs. Then, about eighty years before Cheops' time, Pharaoh Zoser came to the throne. Royal tombs in Zoser's day were rectangular,

An Egyptian serf plowing behind a team of oxen. Nobles often placed models like this in their tombs, believing that magic would bring the serf and oxen to life in the next world, where they would continue to work for their master.

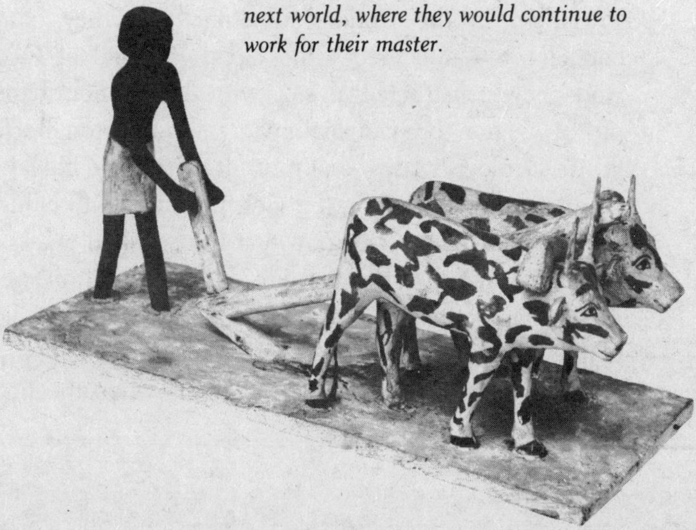

flat-topped structures made of brick. (They are called *mastaba* tombs, after an Arab word meaning bench, which is what they resembled.)

Pharaoh Zoser, knowing that brick crumbled in time, desired a tomb for himself that would last for all eternity. And so his chief architect and vizier, a remarkable man named Imhotep, conceived the idea of building his lord's final resting place entirely of stone.

Imhotep ordered limestone to be quarried from the valley cliffs and cut to the shape and size of bricks. With these stone bricks he built a huge mastaba. On top of it he placed a smaller mastaba, and then a smaller one on top of the second. In all there were six mastabas, one on top of the other. They rose more than two hundred feet into the air, and looked like a giant staircase. This tomb, known as the Step Pyramid, was the first significant structure in the world built entirely of stone. And it was the first pyramid built in Egypt.

Only eighty years later, the valley people had become so skilled in the working of stone that they could conceive of—and erect—the Great Pyramid of Giza. And they constructed it not with little brick-shaped pieces of stone, but with giant two-and-a-half-ton blocks.

Archaeologists know that most of these huge blocks of granite were quarried on the spot, from the cliffs behind the pyramid. They also know that the polished blocks of limestone that sheathed the outside of the pyramid were cut from the cliffs opposite the pyramid, on the other side of the river. This limestone was transported across the Nile during the Inundation each year, when the flood waters enabled the heavy barges to maneuver up to the base of the cliffs.

Archaeologists know, too, that a permanent crew of about 4,000 expert stone masons and sculptors worked at the site all year round. (Traces have been found of the barracks where they lived.) An additional work force of some 95,000 men worked on the pyramid each year, during the four-month period of the Inundation. This was a time of enforced idleness for Egypt's farmers since their fields lay covered by the Nile flood waters. And so Cheops gave them employment—and fed and housed them in the bargain. (Historian James Baikie calls this "the first unemployment scheme on record.") Archaeologists think that Herodotus was not far from the mark when he wrote that it took 1,600 talents—$3,000,000 in modern money—to pay for the radishes, garlic and onions it took to feed these conscripted workers during the twenty years the pyramid was being built.

The barracks of the permanent work force were close to the river. Nearby were the landing stages where the great blocks of stone were unloaded. A causeway of hard-packed stone and rubble led inland from the landing stages to the base of the pyramid. The giant stone blocks had to be transported along the causeway to the pyramid, and in some way hoisted into place—up dizzying heights as the pyramid grew.

But how was this done? The only tools and equipment the pyramid builders possessed were chisels, copper saws, ropes, measuring tapes made of knotted string, sledges and rollers. They had no wheeled carts or wagons of any

The giant sphinx, between Pharaoh Chephren's pyramid tomb (left) and Pharaoh Cheops' Great Pyramid of Giza

kind. They had no cranes, no block and tackle, no lifting equipment of any sort. Herodotus, unreliable though he often was, unfortunately had nothing to say about the actual techniques used in building the pyramid. And no records or tomb paintings have been found that describe or show how the work was done.

Over the years, archaeologists have advanced many theories about how the great stones were raised into place. One (and surely reasonable) theory holds that, first of all, the huge blocks of stone were unloaded and dragged to the workshops near the river front. There they were measured to size with knotted strings, then cut to shape with copper saws. When each stone was ready, it was bound around with ropes and levered up onto rollers, or a sledge. A crew of forty men was then harnessed to the ropes, like horses. When the order was given, they strained forward in unison. They tugged and pulled, bent nearly double, until at last the great stone rocked and moved forward. Inch by inch, the men dragged the cut granite up onto the causeway and along the causeway to the base of the pyramid.

This causeway, so the theory goes, connected with four ramps, built flat against the sides of the pyramid and slanted steeply upward from ground level. Like the causeway, the ramps were made of hard-packed rubble and stone. Up them, the forty-man crews dragged each of the more than two million blocks of stone that went into the body of the pyramid. When the core of the structure was finished, the ramps completely hid the pyramid from its base to its apex.

Next the limestone blocks that sheathed the outside of the pyramid were dragged, one by one, to the top of the structure. Now the work proceeded downward. As each course of limestone was laid, the ramps were lowered one level. When the entire pyramid had been sheathed and the workers had reached ground level, the ramps had been destroyed and Giza stood forth in all its shining majesty.

Close to Cheops' pyramid stood row upon row of mastaba tombs, built by Pharaoh's nobles, favorites and officials. They were clustered close around the resting place of the god-king they hoped to serve in the next world, as they had served him on earth.

Not far from the mastaba tombs stood the pyramid of Cheops' Queen. Nearby was an empty stretch of desert and a great outcropping of tawny rock. Here Cheops' son and heir, Chephren, would one day build a pyramid almost as big as his father's. And he would order his sculptors to transform the rock outcropping into a giant sphinx—a sphinx with the body of a lion and a portrait head of Chephren himself.

Like the great pyramids, Chephren's sphinx has endured over the long centuries. Today, as it did more than 4,500 years ago, it stands in the shadows of the pyramids of Giza, gazing sightlessly out over the Nile toward the rising sun.

In the year 1924 of the present century, a group of archaeologists was excavating among the mastaba tombs around Cheops' Great Pyramid. Quite by chance, in an

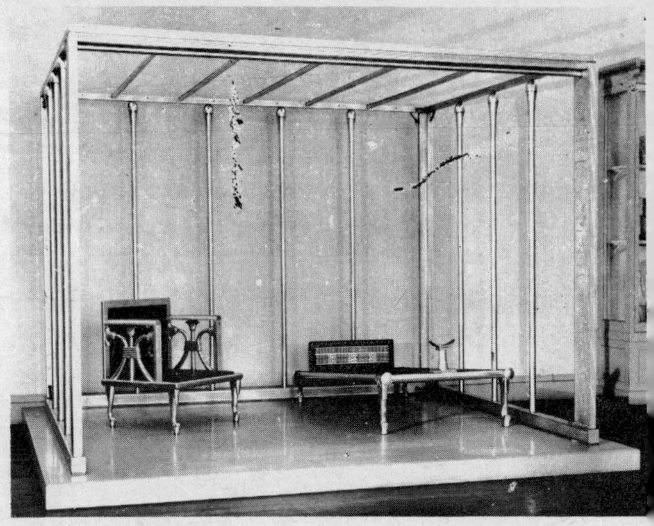

The canopy, bed and chair of Queen Hetephrās, reconstructed from fragments of gold and wood found in her secret burial chamber

Her hand mirror, made of gold and polished bronze

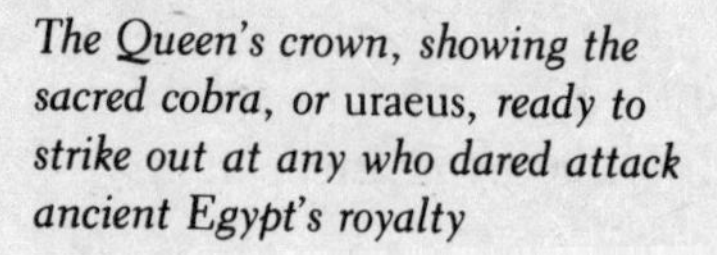

The Queen's crown, showing the sacred cobra, or uraeus, *ready to strike out at any who dared attack ancient Egypt's royalty*

ancient quarry nearby, they stumbled on the blocked-up entrance to a shaft that had been tunneled down into the rock.

The archaeologists stopped everything to explore the underground passage. It slanted down into the darkness for a distance of eighty-five feet and then came up against a stone wall. With infinite care, the excavators pried out one of the stones and stared into pitch-black space beyond. One of the men lit a candle, thrust it into the opening—and caught his breath. By its flickering light he had glimpsed a large white alabaster sarcophagus, and the glitter of gold.

The rest of the wall was hastily removed and the archaeologists crept into the musty underground room. The white sarcophagus stood against the far wall. And the floor in front of it was littered with broken funerary equipment—alabaster and gold jars, pieces of gold leaf, gold lion's paws and pieces of rotted furniture.

One of the segments of gold leaf was covered with hieroglyphs. Using tweezers, the archaeologists gently lifted it up, and read:

"Mother of the King of Upper and Lower Egypt, follower of Horus, guide of the ruler, favorite lady whose every word is done for her, daughter of the god of his body, Hetephras . . ."

Hetephras! The archaeologists who were huddled together in the underground room stared at each other in disbelief. Hetephras, the mother of Cheops, had been buried in her own imposing pyramid at Dashur, just up river from Cairo. Archaeologists had found her tomb empty, and had assumed that it had been robbed in antiquity. How did this great Queen's sarcophagus come to be hidden away in a crude underground chamber at Giza?

With as much haste as their exact science allowed, the archaeologists worked to clear the room of its shattered but priceless treasures. Reaching the sarcophagus at last, they broke its seal, pried the heavy lid upward—and found the coffin empty.

This was an old, old story to archaeologists. Time and again, they had discovered ancient tombs only to find their sarcophagi empty and their funerary equipment gone. For in spite of the awe felt by all ancient Egyptians for their god-kings, the riches buried with Pharaoh were too tempting for the unscrupulous to resist. From the unification of Egypt down to the end of her history, thieves had broken into and robbed the royal tombs—no matter how impregnably they were built, or how cleverly their entrances were camouflaged.

The disappointed archaeologists at Giza guessed that this is what had happened to the mummy of Queen Hetephras. During Cheops' lifetime, they theorized, thieves had broken into her pyramid at Dashur. They had stripped the Queen's mummy of its priceless jewels, and then burned her body. For if the Queen's body were destroyed, her spirit, or *ka*, would be unable to haunt or take vengeance upon the violators of her tomb.

The terrified guards at Dashur had resealed the sarcophagus and then reported the theft to Cheops. In a fury, he ordered his mother's coffin and funerary equipment removed to Giza. There it was to be temporarily reburied, while Cheops built her a new pyramid.

And so a shaft was hastily tunneled into the quarry rock, and Queen Hetephras' sarcophagus was lowered, unopened, into the crude little chamber below. Her funerary equipment was dumped in after her, and the shaft was sealed off.

It was never disturbed again. Possibly Cheops died before he could build a new and fitting tomb for his mother. In any case, he almost surely never knew that her body had been destroyed—a desecration that would have filled him with horror, as it would all Egyptians. For the destruction of a dead person's body ended all hope for eternal life after death.

Certainly Cheops never knew that his own great fortress of a tomb at Giza would be broken into in much the same way—not by modern Arabs, as archaeologists at first supposed, but by his own people. This was to happen not long after Cheops' death, when ancient Egypt sank into a period of near anarchy and despair—a period that archaeologists have called her Dark Ages.

"I Show Thee a Land Topsy-Turvy. . . ."

From about 2553 B.C. to about 1505 B.C.

One night toward the end of the last century, five native thieves were digging in the scrubland near the edge of the Egyptian desert. There was no moon and the men worked as swiftly and silently as shadows. They had been thrusting their spades into the sand for more than two hours when one of the men tensed. His shovel had struck something hard. With a sharp "*Hsst!*" he summoned his companions, and all five men dropped to their knees and began scooping away the sand with their hands.

Moments later the thieves squatted back on their heels to stare down at the object they had uncovered. Then one man laughed, another snorted in disgust and the other three began to curse.

For what they had dug up was a large, mummified crocodile.

Now a mummified crocodile was the last thing in the world the thieves had hoped to find. They were digging for antiquities—a necklace once worn by a Pharaoh's Queen, an offering bowl from a long-vanished temple or the statuette of an ancient Egyptian god. For since the coming of the archaeologists, everyone in Egypt had learned that all sorts of priceless objects lay buried beneath their desert sands.

Most natives were too apathetic to care. But there were a greedy few who began digging recklessly, for profit. Egyptian antiquities had become a fad with collectors the world over. And the natives knew that Cairo dealers would pay them handsomely for a lucky find.

The Egyptian government tried to stop these native diggers by law. Of course it wanted to end their destructive plunder but, more important, it felt that relics from the days of the Pharaohs should go to the Cairo Museum, not to private collectors abroad.

But laws did not stop the natives. They simply went underground and excavated secretly at night. For there were black-market dealers in Cairo's back alleys who would still pay them handsomely for a lucky find.

Now a mummified crocodile was certainly a find, though scarcely a lucky one. For it was much too big to be hidden under a cloak and smuggled into Cairo. So the five thieves dragged the crocodile off to a cave at the desert's edge and burned its leathery old body to a crisp. Then, since the night was still young, they went on digging.

To their disgust, they uncovered another mummified crocodile. Then a third. And a fourth. The thieves dragged these off to the cave and burned them, as they had the first. Then they held a parley.

They had obviously stumbled upon a crocodile

cemetery. In ancient days, crocodiles had been worshiped in certain parts of the Nile Valley. On death, these sacred animals were buried in special cemeteries around a small temple dedicated to Sobk, the crocodile god. Sobk's chapels contained votive offerings of all kinds—amulets, statues and sacred vessels of gold, silver and alabaster.

Prizes such as these, the five thieves knew, would bring a fortune on the black market. So they voted to go on digging in the hope of finding the cemetery chapel, which they knew must lie buried beneath the sand somewhere nearby.

The thieves dug up and burned more than one hundred big mummified crocodiles during the next year. Then at last their patience was rewarded. One night they uncovered the top of the small chapel they had been searching for. Tense with excitement, they cleared away the sand, chopped a hole in the chapel roof and lowered themselves down into the darkness below.

A Nile River crocodile, made of glazed pottery

With shaking fingers the thieves lighted their candles and peered about. On top of a stone altar in the center of the room lay the mummified body of a baby crocodile. Otherwise—nothing. The little chapel was as bare as a bone.

In a fury of rage and disappointment, one of the thieves seized the mummified baby crocodile, swung it up over his head, and smashed it down on the stone altar. Its brittle body broke in half. And out onto the floor tumbled more than half a dozen ancient papyrus scrolls.

The baby crocodile had been stuffed with 2,000-year-old waste paper.

Fortunately (although it is not known how), archaeologists got hold of this waste paper before the thieves could sell it or throw it away as junk. The scrolls turned out to be the day-by-day records kept by the overseer of an Egyptian country estate. They were full of invaluable information about commercial and agricultural life in the days of ancient Egypt's decline.

But imagine the despair of the archaeologists when they learned that one hundred or more big crocodiles had been burned to ashes in the desert cave! For it was reasonable to suppose that they, too, had been stuffed with discarded papyrus scrolls. And who could say how many ancient letters, poems, accounts and temple records had gone up in smoke, lost to archaeology forever.

Papyrus scrolls have turned up in all sorts of unlikely places in Egypt (though in none so unusual as the stomach of a mummified baby crocodile). Archaeologists

Fragment of an ancient papyrus scroll. The script is Hieratic, a kind of longhand version of the hieroglyphs.

have found them clutched in the bony fingers of ancient mummies. They have found them inside half-broken jars, in temple caskets and underneath sand mounds that turned out to be the rubbish heaps of ancient cities. Through these brittle old scrolls, the ancient Egyptians have told archaeologists a great deal about themselves.

Two such scrolls, for example, give a vivid picture of the troubled times that afflicted the valley not long after Pharaoh Cheops' death.

"This land is helter-skelter," read the faded ink on the

first scroll. "I show thee a land topsy-turvy. . . . I show thee the son as foe, the brother as an enemy, and a man killing his father. . . ."

And the second scroll went on:

> The high-born are full of lamentation but the poor are jubilant. Every town sayeth, "Let us drive out the powerful." . . . The splendid judgment hall has been stripped of its documents. . . . The public offices lie open and their records have been stolen. Serfs have become the masters of serfs. . . . Behold, they that had clothes are now in rags. . . . Squalor is throughout the land: no clothes are white these days. . . . The Nile is in flood yet no one has the heart to plow. . . . The dead are thrown in the river. . . . Laughter has perished. Grief walks the land.

Now this sounds very much as though the Egyptian poor had revolted against Pharaoh and seized control of the valley themselves. But archaeologists do not think this is what actually happened. There was certainly a period of disorder and anarchy in Egypt not long after Cheops' death. But it was caused by a revolution among the nobles, not by an uprising of the people.

Perhaps more than any other Pharaoh in Egypt's long history, Cheops seems best to have personified his people's ideal of a great god-king. So far as can be told, the Egyptians worshiped and served him with pride and devotion.

But the Pharaohs who followed Cheops on the throne seem to have lacked his character, strength and dignity. And as one weak Pharaoh succeeded another, the nobles and priests around them grew stronger and bolder. Little by little, these men began to nibble away at their god-king's absolute power.

The priests of the great sun god, Ra, were the first to limit Pharaoh's might. Long considered the wise men of Egypt, these priests had grown in number and influence since unification. When Cheops' dynasty, the fourth, came to an end about fifty years after his death, the priests of Ra were strong enough to put kings of their own choosing on the throne. Pharaoh, they claimed, was henceforth to be considered the son of Ra, and no longer an independent god in his own right. As the earthly representatives of Pharaoh's great father, the sun, the priests of Ra now became powers behind the throne. They began to play an increasingly influential role in the affairs of Egypt, sometimes openly, sometimes behind the scenes.

Pharaoh's once-devoted nobles were the next to defy his absolute authority. Cheops and the earlier Pharaohs had owned all the land in Egypt themselves. They had allotted great estates to their favorites, with the understanding that such estates would revert to the crown on the noble's death. But now these men began to claim that Pharaoh's land grants were theirs by right. Assuming the title *Erapti-hati-a*, or Hereditary Prince, they used the land as they saw fit and willed it on death to their children. With no army to back them up, the Pharaohs who followed Cheops on the throne were powerless to retake their property. And so great feudal estates began to grow up along the banks of the Nile. Each was ruled over by a local prince who grew increasingly hostile to his neighbors and increasingly independent of his king.

These powerful princes at last even dared to challenge Pharaoh's control over their life in the next world—just as they were challenging his control over their lives on earth. The nobles now claimed their right to a life after death, whether Pharaoh needed them to serve him in the next world or not. Life after death, the nobles said, had been promised to every worthy man by Osiris, god of the dead.

Since unification, the cult of the god Osiris had been growing in strength and popularity among the valley people. According to an ancient myth, Osiris had been a god-king of Egypt back at the beginning of time. He had been murdered by his jealous brother and then brought back to life by the powerful magic of his wife, Isis. The resurrected Osiris then became king of the next world, the "First of the Westerners." (For the next world was thought to lie somewhere beyond the setting sun, and those who died were said to have "gone west.")

Osiris ruled from his underworld Judgment Hall. There, the Egyptians had come to believe, an awesome trial awaited every man after his death. After a perilous trip through the dark and demon-filled underworld, the dead man reached the portals of the Judgment Hall and was brought before Osiris. He was then solemnly judged guilty or not guilty of forty-two mortal sins. If he could answer not guilty to all, Osiris would gravely motion him to continue on to the next world. But if the dead man was found guilty of any one of the sins, a great beast

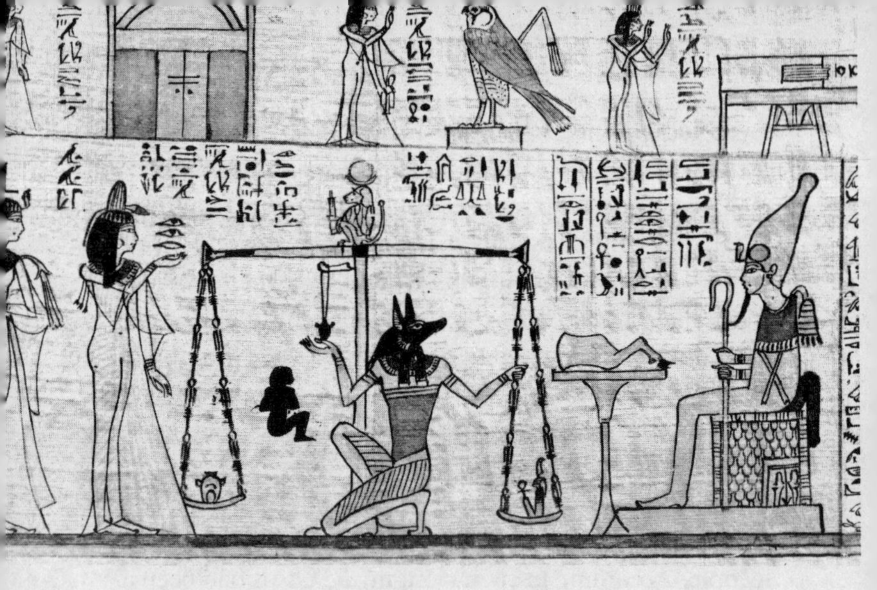

The underworld Judgment Hall of Osiris. The God of the Dead is seated on his throne at the right. A dead princess stands next to the scales as Anubis, the jackal-headed God of Embalming, weighs her heart against the feather of Truth. If the princess has truthfully committed no sins, Osiris will motion her on to the next world.

would pad forward from the shadows, fangs bared—a beast part crocodile, part lion and part hippopotamus. The guilty man would be devoured on the spot, and that would be the end of his hopes for a life everlasting.

Thus, the nobles now claimed, it was not service to Pharaoh that determined whether or not a man lived on after death. It was a man's own worthiness, as judged by Osiris, that decided his fate. And so the nobles ceased building their tombs clustered close around Pharaoh's, as they had done for so many centuries. Instead, they denied their god-king's power over their destiny by building their tombs far from his, in the valley cliffs behind their own estates.

Approximately four hundred years after Cheops' death, the defiant nobles had grown so strong that all central authority in Egypt at last collapsed. The country sank into a period of anarchy, known as her Dark Ages, that lasted for nearly one hundred years.

The valley was torn apart and divided against itself. Little pharaohs, each ruling his own domain along the river, fought their neighbors for land and power. The country's vital irrigation systems fell into disrepair. Periodic famine crippled the valley and lawlessness was widespread. "The land," as the faded scroll had said, was indeed "topsy-turvy."

It was during this time, archaeologists believe, that thieves broke into the Great Pyramid of Giza and robbed Cheops' burial chamber of its jewels, furnishings and statuary. And it was these thieves, too, who probably destroyed Cheops' mummy to avoid the revenge of his ka. For the body of "the Good God" has never been found.

A prince from the little upriver village of Thebes at long last restored order to the valley. He marched against the other barons and subdued them one by one. Then he proclaimed himself Pharaoh of a once-again united Egypt, and transferred the capital from Memphis to his native city in Upper Egypt. The barons, however, were not yet ready to give up the power they had held for so long. They plunged the valley into warfare time and time again. Not until another Theban named Amenemhet seized the throne and founded the powerful Twelfth Dynasty did Egypt once again enjoy lasting peace.

The Twelfth Dynasty was to last for two hundred years. Pharaoh Amenemhet's powerful successors ruled as "the Good Shepherds" of a contented and once-more unified people. Great irrigation projects were undertaken again. Trade, broken off during the feudal period, was resumed with Syria and Palestine. The valley people prospered as they had under Pharaoh Cheops, some five hundred years before.

But then catastrophe struck again. This time the trouble came from outside Egypt's borders.

"A blast of God smote us," wrote the ancient historian Manetho.

> And unexpectedly, from the regions of the East, invaders of obscure race marched in confidence of victory against our land. By main force they easily seized it without striking a blow; and, having overpowered the rulers of the land, they then burned our cities ruthlessly, razed to the ground the temples of the gods, and treated all the natives with a cruel hostility. . . . Finally, they appointed as king one of their number. . . .

These "invaders of obscure race" were the Hyksos of Syria. Some archaeologists believe they filtered into the Delta until they were strong enough to take over the country. Others think they swept down into Egypt as an invading horde—driving horses hitched to chariots, which the astonished Egyptians had never seen before.

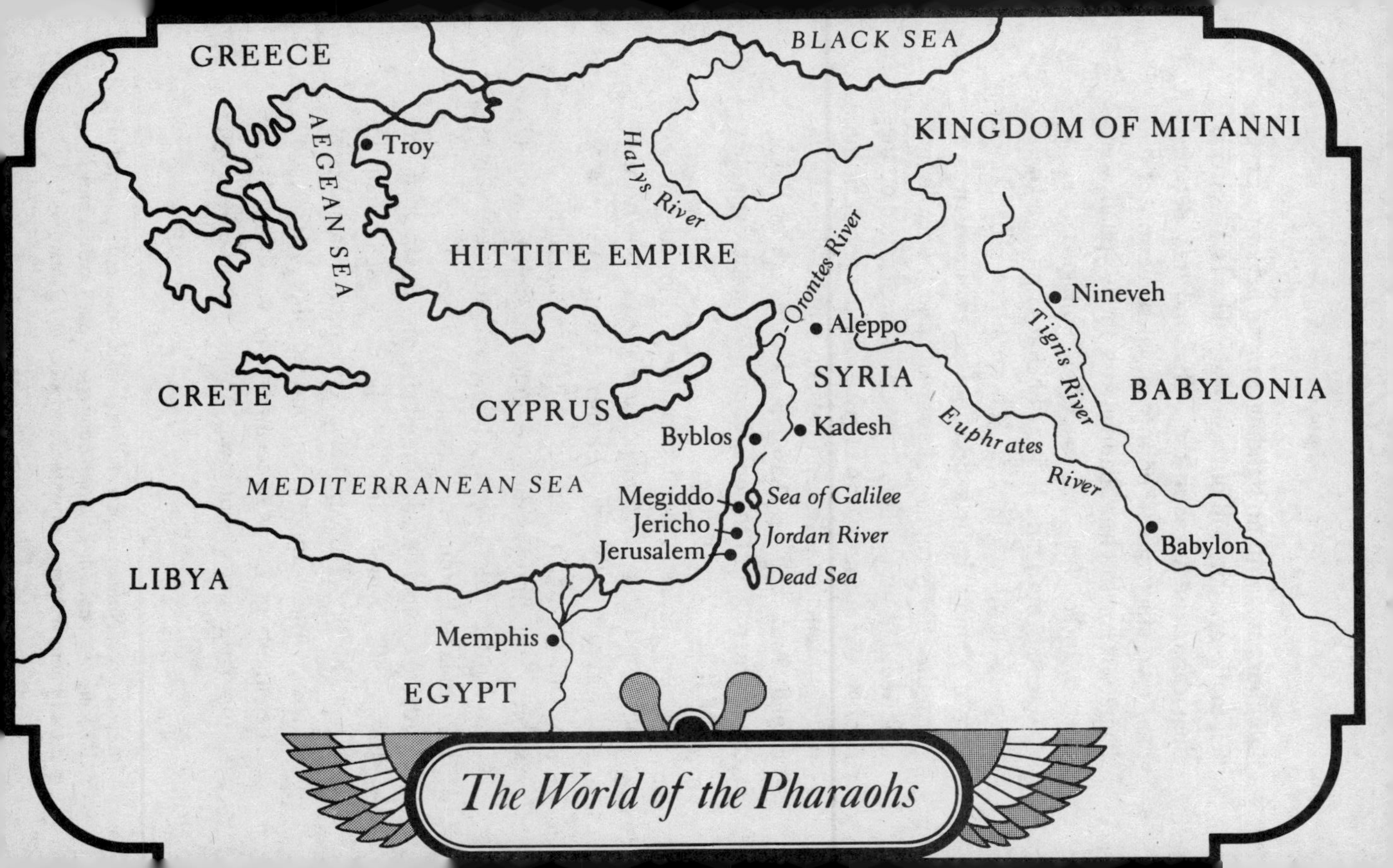
GREECE
BLACK SEA
KINGDOM OF MITANNI
AEGEAN SEA
Troy
Halys River
HITTITE EMPIRE
Orontes River
Nineveh
Aleppo
Tigris River
CRETE
SYRIA
BABYLONIA
CYPRUS
Byblos
Kadesh
Euphrates River
MEDITERRANEAN SEA
Megiddo
Sea of Galilee
Jericho
Jordan River
Jerusalem
Babylon
Dead Sea
LIBYA
Memphis
EGYPT
The World of the Pharaohs

In either case, with no standing army of her own, Egypt fell to the invaders without a struggle. The Hyksos made their capital in Avaris in the Delta, and they declared their own chieftains to be the official successors of the Pharaohs. For 150 humiliating years, the Egyptians were ruled by these "vile" and "wretched" foreigners.

Rescue came again, as it had before, from the Upper Egyptian town of Thebes. There a powerful prince named Kamose built a fleet and sailed down river to storm the enemy capital. He was killed in the battle that followed, but his brother, Prince Ahmose, carried on the fight. It was Ahmose who at last broke the power of the hated conquerors. He captured and burned their Delta capital. And then he chased the Hyksos out of Egypt, driving them across the desert and back to the Syria they had left 150 years before.

While Ahmose was pursuing the Hyksos, the nobles made one last try for independent power. But Ahmose returned and ruthlessly put them down, this time for once and all. During the rest of Egypt's long history, the nobles were almost as subservient to Pharaoh as they had been during Cheops' time. They served him devotedly as his officials at home and abroad.

Ahmose proclaimed himself the first Pharaoh of the Eighteenth Dynasty. It was to be the most brilliant in Egypt's history. The capital was once more established at Thebes. And Ahmose announced that Amon, the Theban city-god, was henceforth to be worshiped as the "King of the Gods." For it was Amon, Ahmose believed,

A company of Nubian archers made of painted wood and discovered in the tomb of an ancient Egyptian army officer. Such soldiers may have helped Pharaoh Ahmose drive the Hyksos out of Egypt.

who had led him to victory against the "vile" Hyksos.

Time and again, the successors of Ahmose had to march against the rebellious Syrians and Nubians. Ahmose's youngest son Thutmose, who became Pharaoh in about 1524 B.C., spent most of his reign in warlike expeditions against the Syrian princelings. He led the valley men farther afield than they had ever ventured before—all the way to the upper reaches of the great Euphrates River. There Thutmose erected a commemorative tablet. For "never," as he truthfully said, "had the like happened to other [Egyptian] kings" before him.

When Thutmose the First died, he was buried in an underground tomb in a desolate valley behind the western cliffs opposite Thebes. Known as the Valley of the Kings, this eerie spot was to be the royal burying ground for centuries to come. The days of pyramid building had passed.

Almost 1,000 years had now gone by since Pharaoh Cheops sat upon the golden throne of Egypt. Yet a serf or a noble from Cheops' time would have felt quite at home in Thutmose the First's Egypt.

It is true that the capital had been transferred to Thebes, and that Memphis was no longer the center of valley life. The temples were perhaps more imposing, and the priests more numerous. Osiris now reigned supreme in the world beyond. And a little local god named Amon of Thebes had become the great state god of Egypt.

But otherwise little had changed. The three seasons of

flood, planting and harvest went on as they had from time immemorial, surrounded by the same anxieties and ceremonies. Life at court, and in the villages and on the great country estates had scarcely changed in ten long centuries. The craftsmen and field workers of Thutmose the First's day plied their trades and planted their crops with the very same techniques used in Cheops' day. Even fashion had not changed. The men and women of the nobility wore the same sort of wigs, make-up, jewelry and clothing that had been worn 1,000 years earlier —except that their linen kilts and sheaths were now sometimes finely pleated.

And yet there were differences. The upheavals of the last 1,000 years had taught the valley people two lessons that they would never forget.

The time of anarchy under the feudal barons had convinced them of the vital need for a strong central government, under a Pharaoh whose divine authority must never again be questioned. And the Hyksos invasion had taught them that their isolated valley was not safe from attack after all. Egypt was never again to be without an army. And she came to feel that her only safety lay in subduing the nations around her, so that none among them could ever invade the valley again.

"His Majesty, Herself" —Queen Hatshepsut

From about 1505 B.C.
to about 1484 B.C.

On the western banks of the Nile, opposite the site of ancient Thebes, stand the ruins of the most beautiful temple in all Egypt. Known today as Deir el Bahri, the temple was once called *Zeser zesru*, the Holy of Holies. It was the mortuary chapel of Thutmose the First's daughter—Her Royal (and mysterious) Highness, Queen Hatshepsut. She was, according to Egyptologist James Henry Breasted, "The first great woman in history of whom we are informed."

Deir el Bahri is cut directly into the face of the yellow limestone cliffs that border the valley on the west. Three broad terraces, rising one above the other, lead from the desert up to its columned entrance. In Hatshepsut's day, these terraces were planted with fragrant incense trees. And the wide processional way that led across each level was bordered with sandstone and pink granite sphinxes. Each sphinx had the body of a lion and the head and face of Hatshepsut—with a false granite beard attached to her delicate, pointed chin.

Archaeologists found these bearded sphinxes in an ancient quarry near the temple. They had been dumped there thousands of years before—after being savagely smashed to bits.

Not long after this, archaeologists made another puzzling find at Deir el Bahri. In front of the temple's lowest terrace, they discovered the hidden entrance to a secret passageway. It led deep underground to a small burial chamber directly beneath the innermost sanctuary of Hatshepsut's chapel. Here, too, everything had been ruthlessly destroyed. From mutilated inscriptions on the walls, archaeologists learned that the tomb had belonged to a man named Senmut, chief architect to the Queen.

From the evidence of Hatshepsut's shattered sphinxes and the wreckage in Senmut's tomb, it was clear that a scene of violence and hatred had once taken place in serene and lovely Deir el Bahri.

Just why that violence had taken place became clear as archaeologists pieced together Hatshepsut's story. It was one of the most dramatic in ancient Egyptian history. For it was the story of a beautiful woman who stole the throne of Egypt from a child and ruled in uneasy peace for twenty-one years—until that child grew to manhood and, presumably, destroyed her.

Hatshepsut's story has been called the Feud of the Thutmosids by archaeologists. For it began with a tangle of family relationships that may have had much to do with what happened later.

To begin with, Thutmose the First had four children by his Great Royal Wife. All died in childhood, except

Deir el Bahri, Queen Hatshepsut's mortuary chapel, beneath the western cliffs opposite Thebes

the little Princess Hatshepsut. Thutmose also had a son by one of his secondary wives. (By custom, the Pharaohs of ancient Egypt kept harems and married secondary wives in addition to their official Queens.)

It was also the custom in ancient Egypt for royal brothers and sisters to marry each other. This kept the throne in the family, so to speak, and preserved the purity of the dynastic line. Hatshepsut, however, had no royal brother. And so, the next best thing was arranged for her. When Thutmose the First felt his end drawing near, he married Hatshepsut to her half-brother, his son by a secondary wife. When Thutmose died, this man became Pharaoh Thutmose the Second, and Hatshepsut was the Queen of Egypt. She was now in her late teens, a slim and lovely girl with almond-shaped eyes and a small, firm mouth.

Hatshepsut and her handsome but sickly husband had two little daughters. In addition, Thutmose the Second had a son by a woman in his harem. When this boy was about nine years old, the court physicians told Thutmose the Second that he had not long to live. Since the royal family was again without a crown prince, Thutmose married his tiny elder daughter to his son by the harem woman. On Thutmose's death, this sturdy boy became Thutmose the Third, and his tiny bride the Great Royal Wife. Hatshepsut, now in her early twenties, was relegated to the role of Dowager Queen Mother —although she had been named one of a group of regents to govern Egypt until Thutmose the Third was old enough to rule alone.

Theoretically, Hatshepsut should now have stepped into the background. And, indeed, for the next few years that is just what she seemed to do. She walked submissively behind the boy-Pharaoh on all state occasions.

And she deferred in every way to her little daughter, the Queen.

But during all this time, she was apparently gathering the reins of government more and more firmly into her own slim fingers. For soon, according to one of her father's old courtiers: "Hatshepsut carried on the affairs of The Two Lands according to her own ideas. Egypt was made to work in submission to her . . . the Lady of Command, whose plans are excellent, who satisfies the Two Regions when she speaks."

But to govern Egypt in the name of young Thutmose the Third did not satisfy Hatshepsut. She wanted something more.

And so one day (the records do not say when or how) Hatshepsut must have donned the most sacred of Pharaoh's official costumes—a ceremonial dress that went back to the predynastic kings of Egypt. Wearing, then, only a short kilt with a lion's tail hanging to the ground in back, carrying the royal scepter in one hand and the sacred flail, or crook, in the other—and with a square-cut false beard attached to her chin—Hatshepsut mounted the throne and proclaimed herself Pharaoh of Egypt.

So far as can be told, no one opposed her—openly. And thus, in a bloodless *coup d'état* (seizure of power), Hatshepsut became the first woman to rule over the Nile Valley—or "His Majesty herself," as the confused chroniclers were often to call her.

Personal ambition may have driven Hatshepsut to seize the throne. But she was a woman of fierce family

Amon, King of the Gods (at right), bestowing his blessing on Queen Hatshepsut. The relief sculpture appears on an obelisk of Queen Hatshepsut.

pride, too. Her father had been the mighty Thutmose the First. Her grandfather, Ahmose the Liberator, had driven the Hyksos from Egypt and founded the Eighteenth Dynasty. The purest of royal blood flowed through Hatshepsut's veins—whereas the boy Pharaoh, Thutmose the Third, was very nearly a commoner. Son of a harem nobody and Hatshepsut's husband, who was only half-royal himself, little Thutmose the Third could claim to be only one-quarter royal. Hatshepsut passionately believed that she alone, by blood and birth, was entitled to the throne—irrespective of the fact that she was a woman.

Her deep conservatism showed itself in another way. Hatshepsut mistrusted the foreign entanglements and conquests of her father, Thutmose the First. Egypt, she felt, should withdraw from the world outside its borders and return to the peaceful, valley-bound days of its past. Except for trading expeditions, the country should turn its back on the wretched foreigner, and let him go his quarrelsome and barbaric way alone.

There were many, in tradition-bound Egypt, who agreed with her. The High Priest of Amon was one, along with many of his priesthood. And many of Egypt's most powerful and important nobles feared and distrusted their country's involvement with the world outside Egypt's borders.

These people became Hatshepsut's devoted supporters, both before and after she seized the throne. But she had many enemies, too. Some of the Amon priests saw in foreign conquest a chance to enrich their temple and to make Amon the most powerful god in the world. The army, with its vested interest in war, opposed her. So, too, did many nobles and officials. Some were merely scandalized at the idea of a woman Pharaoh. Others dreamed of an Egypt that would control the eastern Mediterranean world. And still others believed that the only protection from another invasion like the Hyksos' lay in the ruthless suppression of the warring countries outside Egypt's borders. All of these were supporters of the boy Pharaoh, Thutmose the Third.

But they were not strong enough to depose Hatshepsut. She seized the throne—and held it. For the next twenty-one years she ruled Egypt unopposed. But it could not have been an easy time for her. Underneath the surface calm, her court must have seethed with intrigue.

An English artist named Winifred Brunton painted a portrait of Hatshepsut for her book *Kings and Queens of Ancient Egypt*. As she worked, using ancient sculptures as a guide, the artist wrote that:

> Into her portrait as Queen there crept, almost without my will, a look of watchfulness, or even suspicion under its calm. In the . . . position she occupied, against precedent in a country where precedent was justification in itself, and amid so many enemies and spies, she must have felt perpetually insecure, even though her immediate entourage was ardently devoted to her.

The moment she seized the throne, Hatshepsut ordered Thutmose the Third banished to the vast and gloomy interior of the temple of Amon. There his head was shaved and his royal garments were exchanged for a simple linen kilt. He was put into training as an apprentice priest, and the court saw him no more. His little bride was presumably sent back to the palace nursery.

Next, Hatshepsut appointed the loyal High Priest of

Amon to be her vizier. And with his help she set about restoring the temples of Egypt. They had fallen into grievous disrepair during the long rule of the Hyksos.

"Listen to me, all men!—you folk, as many as there are of you!" she cried.

> I have restored that which was in ruins, and I have raised up that which had been left [lying] since . . . the foreign barbarians were in your midst . . . ruling in ignorance of Ra. Nothing was done . . . until the time when My Majesty was established upon the throne of Ra. . . . Then I came . . . flaming with indignation . . . and I removed this insult to the great god.

In the meantime, Hatshepsut had begun work at Thebes on her mortuary chapel, Deir el Bahri. It was designed and built for her by her chief architect, Senmut—the one man, so far as can be told, whom Hatshepsut ever loved. Tall and handsome, Senmut had apparently served as a soldier in the army of the Queen's father, Thutmose the First. Where and how he and Hatshepsut met is unknown. But soon he was living in the royal palace, and he and the Queen had become inseparable. Hatshepsut showered him with favors and titles, and his influence was such that her enemies called him the uncrowned Pharaoh of Egypt.

While he was supervising the building of Deir el Bahri, Senmut ordered a secret tomb dug for himself deep beneath Hatshepsut's innermost sanctuary. He wished, gossip later said, to be close for all eternity to the woman he could never marry in life. But the secret was soon out. One day the exact location of Senmut's hidden tomb must have been whispered into the ear of a young apprentice priest who had once been known as Pharaoh Thutmose the Third.

Before Deir el Bahri was completed—and about nine years after Hatshepsut had seized the throne—the Queen organized a great trading expedition to the Land of Punt. The god Amon himself, she said, had commanded her to do so, ordering "that the ways of Punt

Queen Hatshepsut

should be searched out" again, and that incense trees should be brought back from its distant shores for the terraces of Deir el Bahri.

Since the long-ago days of Pharaoh Cheops, Egypt had obtained the incense used in her temples from the Land of Punt (believed to have been on the coast of present-day Somalia). But all trade with that distant country had ceased when the Hyksos invaded the valley some two hundred years earlier. Hatshepsut wanted to reestablish relations with Punt as part of her policy of prosperity through trade instead of through conquest. And so, having received a command from Amon "to do what she had already made up her mind to do"—as James Baikie says in his *History of Egypt*—she ordered five seagoing barges outfitted for the long voyage.

The Queen and all of Thebes gathered at the dock side to watch the big ships move off down the Nile. The expedition's adventures were later pictured in relief on the walls of Deir el Bahri for all to see.

When the Egyptians at last sighted the shores of Punt, the inhabitants hurried to the waterfront to stare in amazement.

"Why have ye come hither unto this land, which the people know not?" they asked with great astonishment. "Did ye come down upon the ways of heaven, or did ye sail upon the waters?"

The Egyptian captain explained that they had come upon the waters. And then he bowed low as the Chief of the Puntites came solemnly forward, accompanied by his enormously fat wife, who rode astride a sadly overburdened little donkey. Tables were set up beneath the trees, and the Egyptians unloaded their trading goods—linen, jewelry, weapons and pottery. A brisk bartering began. And soon the Egyptian ships were bulging with the marvels of the country of Punt: heaps of myrrh gum, living myrrh trees, ebony and pure ivory, green gold, cinnamon wood, incense, eye paint, apes, monkeys, dogs and skins of the southern panther, as well as natives and their children.

Thus heavily laden, the five Egyptian ships set sail for home "with joy of heart." For "never was brought the like of this for any king who has been since the beginning."

Hatshepsut and a great crowd of Thebans were at the dock to greet the returning ships. The Queen watched the unloading all day long, exclaiming in delight as each "marvel" was brought ashore. She ordered the living myrrh trees to be taken directly to Deir el Bahri and planted on the terraces there. Then she offered the expedition's entire cargo to Amon.

That night the Queen gave a great banquet at the royal palace. Flaming oil, burning in high braziers, lighted the vast, columned reception hall. Dancing girls and musicians moved among the many little tables, and waiters hurried to and fro with napkins folded neatly over their arms. The lords of the court and their ladies, with lotus blossoms in their hair, feasted on soup and grilled fish, gazelle steaks and roast duck, cucumber and watercress salad, with fruit and little cakes for dessert.

Flushed and happy, Hatshepsut sat upon a dais with

Senmut on her right and the captain of the expedition on her left. When the feasting was done, the Queen delivered a speech. She had done as Amon had commanded, she said. The ways of Punt had been searched out and the incense trees Amon had desired now stood planted upon the terraces of Deir el Bahri, the temple she had dedicated to her divine father.

"I have made for him a Punt in . . . Thebes, just as he commanded me," she concluded proudly. ". . . It is big enough for him to walk about in."

It may have been at this time or much earlier in her reign—no one knows—that an extraordinary scene took place in Amon's great temple of Karnak.

There, during all these years (so far as is known), Thutmose the Third had been living in obscurity as a minor priest. His name was never mentioned in Hatshepsut's presence; she obviously preferred to think him dead. But Thutmose had many secret partisans among the nobility, the army, and the very priests of Amon with whom he lived.

It was these priests who one day openly dared to show that they believed Thutmose to be the rightful Pharaoh of Egypt. It happened during a solemn ceremony in the temple.

The image of Amon usually rested in the darkened Holy of Holies at Karnak. But on ceremonial days, the statue of the god was placed in a carrying chair shaped like a golden boat, with a cabin in the center. In this vessel, the statue of Amon was carried solemnly around the temple's great hall by a group of priests.

One day the entire court was assembled at Karnak for just such a ceremony. Thutmose the Third was standing in the background, unnoticed by the crowd. In a sudden hush, the white-garbed priests appeared, bearing Amon's golden bark on their shoulders. And then (as Thutmose later described it):

> The god made the circuit of the hall on both sides of it, searching for My Majesty in every place, though the hearts of those who were in front did not comprehend his actions. On recognizing me, he halted—I threw myself on the pavement, I prostrated myself in his presence. . . .

Then, in full sight of everyone, the priests were seen to bend forward. And the golden boat of Amon, with the god seated in the cabin, bowed low before Thutmose. In no clearer way could the great god indicate that he felt Thutmose to be the rightful Pharaoh of Egypt.

Hatshepsut's power at this time was unassailable, and the High Priest of Amon was still her vizier. But the audacity of the dissident priests must have frightened and infuriated her, nonetheless. For not long afterward she did a vengeful thing. To commemorate Amon's choice of *herself* as heir to the throne, she ordered two giant obelisks to be quarried at Aswan. When these needlelike monuments, each about one hundred feet high, arrived in Thebes, Hatshepsut had them sheathed in electrum, a combination of gold and silver. And then she ordered them erected in the very hall where Amon's bark had

bowed low before Thutmose. To raise them into place, the roof of the chamber had to be torn off, making the great hall unfit for further ceremonial use.

When the obelisks were installed Hatshepsut said:

> O ye people who shall see my monument in after years . . . beware lest ye say, "I know not, I know not why this was done—a monument fashioned entirely from gold as if it were an everyday occurrence." I swear as Ra loves me, as my father Amon favors me [that] these two great obelisks, which My Majesty hath wrought with electrum for my father Amon, that my name may abide in this temple eternally, are of one block of enduring granite without seam or joining. . . . The ignorant, like the wise, knoweth it. Let not him who shall hear this say that what I have said is a lie, but rather let him say: "How like her it is! She was truthful in the sight of her father. . . ."

Amon knew of her truthfulness, Hatshepsut concluded. "He caused that I should reign over the Black Land and the Red Land as a reward therefor. I have no enemy in any land. . . ."

Hatshepsut ruled Egypt for twenty-one years. And she ruled it well. Her reign, in spite of its undercurrents of enmity and intrigue, was a tranquil interlude between the old, valley-bound Egypt which traded peaceably with her neighbors, and the new Egypt that was coming—an Egypt of war, conquest, empire and wealth beyond imagining.

Hatshepsut's end came abruptly—and mysteriously. She may have died a normal death. Some archaeologists think so. Others believe that Thutmose at last broke free

Obelisk of Queen Hatshepsut
in Amon's temple of Karnak at Thebes

of Karnak, reseized the throne and brutally murdered the woman who had kept him a virtual prisoner for so long.

Thutmose was now thirty years old. Whether or not he murdered Hatshepsut, he tried to destroy all memory of her in Egypt. He caused her name to be obliterated everywhere it appeared at Deir el Bahri. He ordered her pink granite sphinxes smashed to bits. And Senmut's tomb beneath the Queen's innermost sanctuary was raided and destroyed.

Then, his fury spent, Thutmose turned his attention to a more important matter. Egypt faced invasion once again. Commanded by the prince of a town called Kadesh, 330 Syrian princes and their forces were making ready to challenge the might of the unknown man who now sat on the golden throne of the Pharaohs.

The Smiter of the Asiatics —Pharaoh Thutmose the Third

From about 1484 B.C. to about 1461 B.C.

In a matter of months after Hatshepsut's death, Pharaoh Thutmose the Third was ready "to smite" the rebellious Syrian princelings. He had recruited an army of twenty thousand men and brought them together in a sprawling camp outside the Egyptian frontier fortress of Zaru, in the eastern Delta. There his barefooted infantrymen were armed with swords, shields, and bows and arrows. His charioteers were issued javelins and daggers. And his army's heavy, ox-drawn supply wagons were loaded with beer, bread and extra equipment for the long march ahead.

At last all was ready. Pharaoh's advance scouts and spies slipped out of camp one dark night. And a few days later the army was under way.

To the call of trumpets, the troops filed out through

the gates of Zaru and onto the great commercial road that followed the Mediterranean coast northward into Palestine and Syria. In the lead was a single chariot carrying the standard of Amon—a golden ram's head crowned with a shining disk that represented the sun. Behind Amon's escort marched the royal bodyguards. And then came Thutmose himself. He was driving his own war chariot, his sturdy body braced against the pull of its high-strung team of black stallions. On his head, the blue-leather war helmet of the Pharaohs glinted like steel in the bright sunlight.

Team after team of chariots followed him, their excited horses held down to a trot. Then came the foot soldiers, stretching back along the road for miles and kicking up a great cloud of dust as they moved along. Bringing up the rear were the supply wagons, lumbering along behind their teams of patient white oxen.

Once they were beyond the frontiers of Egypt, Pharaoh gave his troops little rest. In twenty days he marched them across the desert, up into the green lowlands of Palestine and northward to the town of Yehem, in the foothills of the Carmel Mountains. There his advance scouts and spies were waiting for him with important news.

The Prince of Kadesh and his Syrian forces were encamped in front of the fortified city of Megiddo, on the other side of the mountain. There were three routes Pharaoh could follow into Megiddo. One led around the base of the mountain to the left, a second around the

History's first great general,
Pharaoh Thutmose the Third

mountain's base to the right. Both were excellent roads, wide and safe from ambush. There was also a third route, much shorter but extremely dangerous. This was a narrow pass that led directly up over the mountain and down the other side.

Thutmose summoned his commanders and held a council of war. Which of the three routes should the army take into Megiddo? Without hesitation, his officers advised against the mountain pass, as had the scouts.

"How should we go by this road which is narrow and risky?" they asked. "Our scouts . . . tell us that the enemy is waiting there for us, ready to hold the way against any multitude." The troops would have to march single file over the pass, unable to protect themselves from ambush.

". . . Will not horse have to come behind horse and man behind man likewise?" the officers asked. "Shall our vanguard be fighting while our rear guard . . . cannot yet get into action? There are yet two other roads. . . . Let our Victorious Lord march by the road he chooses, but let him not oblige us to go by this difficult road."

This was sound military advice. But Thutmose rejected it impatiently.

"I swear, as Ra loves me and my father Amon praises me," he said, "that My Majesty will proceed [along the mountain pass]. Let him who will among you go upon those roads ye have mentioned, and let him who will among you come in the following of My Majesty. Shall they think, among those enemies whom Ra detests: 'Does His Majesty proceed upon another road? He begins to be frightened of us.' So they will think."

There was no further discussion. With Thutmose in the lead, the army started single file up the mountain pass. And Pharaoh and his vanguard reached the mountain top and encamped there for the night while the main body of his army was still far below.

From the heights the next day Thutmose could look down on the city of Megiddo. The enemy's scouts had warned of Pharaoh's approach, and the Syrians were ready and waiting. In the green plain below, their charioteers and foot soldiers were drawn up in battle formation. The sun glanced off their war helmets, their emblazoned shields and the sleek hides of their powerful war horses. Behind the Syrian army, the gates of Megiddo were closed. And on the ramparts atop the city's walls, the townspeople stood massed and silent, looking anxiously toward the mountain.

Pharaoh did not hesitate at the sight of the formidable army below. Without pausing for the rest of his troops to catch up with him, he started down the mountain side, his vanguard trailing after him in a long, untidy line.

And now occurred the first absurdity of a most absurd battle. The Syrians watched Pharaoh come down onto the plain. They watched him choose a site and make camp. They watched the men of his vanguard straggle in behind him—and they did not attack. If they had, Thutmose would surely have been captured or killed, and Egyptian history might have taken a very different turn.

But no Syrian command was given. No Syrian charge

was made. The enemy watched, without moving, as Thutmose settled in for the night. And when darkness fell, the enemy retired to their tents, allowing most of Pharaoh's army to come down the mountain during the night and join him in camp. By dawn, the Egyptian army in the plain was almost at full strength.

The Battle of Megiddo—the first battle in history of which there is a detailed record—began at daylight the next morning. The Egyptians and Syrians faced each other across the open plain. And, as on the day before, the anxious townspeople of Megiddo stood massed atop the city's walls.

As the sun rose, a single trumpet shrilled in the Egyptian camp. Pharaoh, resplendent in full battle dress, thrust aside the flap of the royal pavilion and strode to his waiting war chariot. Grasping the reins in one hand, he turned to face his waiting charioteers and his eager ranks of foot soldiers. Then he flung up one arm. A great shout filled the quiet morning air. The charioteers' nervous horses reared, and lunged forward into a gallop. With Thutmose, "like a flame of fire," in the lead, the massed chariots swept forward across the plain. Behind them, their shouts drowned out by the thundering hoofs, raced the foot soldiers, swords drawn and at the ready.

And now occurred the second absurdity of the Battle of Megiddo. The Syrians stood as if paralyzed while the Egyptians swept toward them. Then suddenly, without lifting a lance or fitting arrow to bow, they broke ranks and fled. In panic and pandemonium they turned and made for the gates of Megiddo.

Eighteenth-Dynasty relief sculpture showing Egyptian chariots and horses

The astonished Egyptians reined in their snorting horses, the foot soldiers stumbled to a halt and the entire army was treated to a sight it would never forget. The prudent townspeople of Megiddo had locked the city gates before the battle began. Unable to get inside, the frantic Syrians raced about beneath the walls, shouting for help to the watchers above. The Megiddians, equally panic-stricken, began tearing off their clothing, including their underwear. Tying these garments into ropes, they lowered them over the walls and hauled the Syrians, dancing like puppets on strings, up to safety on the ramparts.

If the Egyptians had been less amused—or less greedy—they could have taken Megiddo then and there. But the fleeing Syrians had dropped most of their weapons, and had left their war chariots and richly furnished tents unprotected on the field.

At the sight of this booty, the Egyptian troops ran riot. Neither Pharaoh nor his commanders could control them. They plundered far into the night, thrusting inlaid Syrian daggers through their belts, ripping down the rich hangings in the enemy's tents and making off with the abandoned gold and silver plate and the clothing, ornaments and jewels.

When there was nothing left to plunder, the exhausted and treasure-laden troops were brought before Pharaoh. He sat upon a throne in front of the royal pavilion, his face stern in the flickering torchlight. If his army had taken Megiddo when the enemy broke ranks and fled, he said, all Syria would now be in Egyptian hands.

"Had ye captured this city afterward, behold I would have given [many sacrifices to] Ra this day; because every chief of every country that has revolted is within it; and because it is the capture of a thousand cities, this capture of Megiddo."

It was true enough. The princes of Syria, with their families and retainers, were now safely barricaded behind the walls of Megiddo. The only recourse was to lay siege to the city and starve the enemy into submission. This the Egyptians did. And after several weeks, their food and water gone, the Syrians surrendered. As Thutmose later described it:

> Then that fallen one [the Prince of Kadesh], together with the chiefs who were with him, caused all their children to come forth to My Majesty with many products of gold and silver, all their horses with their trappings, their great chariots of gold and silver with their painted equipment, all their battle armor, their bows, their arrows and all their implements of war—those things, indeed, with which they had come to fight against My Majesty. And now they brought them as tribute to My Majesty while they stood on their walls giving praise to My Majesty. . . .
>
> Then My Majesty caused them to swear an oath, saying: "Never again will we do evil against [Thutmose the Third]—may he live forever—our Lord, in our lifetime, for we have witnessed his power. . . ."
>
> Then My Majesty allowed to them the road to their cities, and they went, all of them, on donkeys. For I had taken their horses, and I carried off their citizens to Egypt and their property likewise.

And thus, having spared the lives of his enemies and sent them home in humiliation on the backs of donkeys, Thutmose broke camp and headed back for Egypt.

The victorious army reached Thebes early in October. News of Pharaoh's return had swept up river before him and the entire capital was waiting to greet him. As Thutmose paraded his troops and his booty through the crowded streets, the Thebans stared dumfounded. For Pharaoh had come home with 2,000 Syrian horses, 924 enemy war chariots, 1,921 Asiatic bulls, 2,000 small cattle, 20,500 additional animals and almost 2,000 prisoners of war. It was these last that caused most comment. The Thebans pursed their lips as eighty-seven wide-eyed sons and daughters of the Syrian princes passed by. (Thutmose had brought them down into Egypt as hostages for their fathers' good behavior.) The little princes and princesses were followed by 1,796 nonroyal male and female prisoners, destined to work as slaves in the temples and at court. As the Syrians shuffled by, manacled together, the Thebans did not trouble to hide their distaste. The prisoners had swarthy complexions, bearded faces and wore multicolored woolen clothing. They seemed "abominable" to the clean-shaven Egyptians, who wore nothing but spotless white linen.

Days of feasting followed Pharaoh's triumphant return, climaxed by a great ceremony at Karnak. There, in gratitude to Amon for leading him to victory, Thutmose presented most of the Syrian booty to the King of the Gods and his priesthood. He gave Amon three Syrian towns with sole right to the tribute therefrom—the tribute that all conquered towns from now on had to pay Pharaoh each year. And he gave the temple extensive lands in Lower and Upper Egypt, which he stocked with the captured herds of Syrian cattle. These rich gifts were the beginning of Amon's vast fortune. It was to grow over the years until the wealth and power of the King of the Gods rivaled that of Pharaoh himself.

Thutmose the Third's first campaign set a pattern that he was to follow for the next twenty years.

Each spring, after the Egyptian harvests were in, he set forth at the head of his army. During his early years as Pharaoh, Thutmose had "to smite" the rebellious

Syrians time and time again. But their small, independent city-states were no match for the unified might of Egypt. Over the years, Thutmose conquered all of Palestine, all of Syria and the trading cities along the Phoenician coast. He warred north of Syria, in the land of a powerful people called the Mitanni. And he campaigned south of Egypt, bringing all of Nubia under Egyptian control.

And when he was done, Thutmose was Pharaoh of an empire that stretched from the headwaters of the Tigris and Euphrates rivers all the way south to the Fourth Cataract of the Nile. His name was feared and his word was law throughout the eastern Mediterranean world—and beyond. The rulers of distant Crete and Babylonia hastened to send rich gifts to the invincible warrior-king who now sat upon the throne of the Pharaohs.

Thutmose ruled his vast empire with a light hand. He established Egyptian garrisons and administrative districts throughout the conquered lands. But his vassal states were allowed to govern themselves much as they pleased—as long as they sent their annual tribute of gold, produce and livestock to Pharaoh's warehouses each year.

Thutmose continued to bring the younger sons and daughters of the Syrian princes down into Egypt with him after each campaign. They were educated at court with his own children and the sons and daughters of the nobility. Many of the little Syrian princesses stayed on in Egypt to become the brides of court nobles. And the young Syrian princes became so Egyptianized (as

Chapel of Thutmose the Third

Thutmose had hoped) that, when they returned to their native cities, they ruled there more as Pharaoh's ambassadors than as his vassals.

Toward the end of his military career, Thutmose's power and reputation were so great that his annual campaigns were little more than military parades. Preceded by his heralds, Pharaoh marched his veteran troops along the dusty roads and byways of the Middle

East. The richness of his retinue dazzled all beholders. And the mere sight of his enormous army was enough to deter the vassal states from raising voice or finger against Egypt's might.

Days of feasting and thanksgiving to Amon followed Pharaoh's return to the valley each fall. Thutmose continued to shower the King of the Gods with wealth. He enlarged Karnak and built a botanical garden and zoo within its precincts. These he filled with rare foreign plants, trees, flowers and wild animals that he collected on his campaigns abroad. In his few moments of leisure, he designed exquisite bowls and vessels for temple use.

During the mild Egyptian winter, Thutmose devoted himself to his many projects at home. Accompanied by his royal architects and engineers—and by his pet baboon—he voyaged from one end of the valley to the other on an annual tour of inspection. He conferred with each of his local governors to make sure all went well in their provinces. He presided at the opening of the new canals and irrigation projects he had instigated. And he visited the more than thirty sites along the river where his architects were restoring old temples or building new ones. He was as tireless, energetic and able a ruler as he was a general.

"Lo, His Majesty was one who knew what happened," said his proud vizier, Rekhmire. "There was nothing of which he was ignorant. He was Thoth [the Egyptian god of Wisdom] in everything; there was no matter which he did not carry out."

At court, Thutmose received a constant stream of

ambassadors and couriers from all corners of his far-flung empire. Some came on state business. Others came bringing the rich tribute that now poured into Egypt from the eastern Mediterranean world and Africa. Week in and week out, foreign ships put in at the Theban port with cargoes destined for Pharaoh's treasury.

One day it would be the Nubians, tall and black. Their bearers padded through the city streets toward the Royal Precinct, carrying ebony, ostrich feathers and ivory upon their backs. Behind them came their herders, calling out to one another in their strange tongue as they drove their skittish cattle through the narrow alleys to Pharaoh's stockyards.

Another day it would be the Asiatics, bringing thoroughbred horses for the royal stables, war chariots, pottery and great bales of grain and fruit. As the years went by, the once wide-eyed Thebans grew so accustomed to the exotic sights in their streets that they scarcely looked up from their workbenches as the riches of the eastern world passed by outside.

Thutmose the Third's wife, Hatshepsut's tiny elder daughter, had died when very young. Pharaoh had then married her sister, who had given him a fine and vigorous son. As Thutmose neared sixty, he made this twenty-year-old boy co-ruler with him of Egypt and her empire. A year later, Thutmose was dead.

"Lo, the King completed his lifetime of many years, splendid in might, in valor and triumph," said one of his grieving generals. "He mounted to heaven, he joined the sun, the divine limbs mingling with him who begat him."

Like his grandfather before him, Thutmose the Third was buried in an underground tomb in the desolate Valley of the Kings. With him was buried the embalmed body of his pet baboon.

Thutmose was history's first great general. He left his mark upon the ancient world. And he changed the course of Egyptian history—for better or worse. From the day that he marched forth "to smite" the Asiatics, Egypt's peaceful days of relative isolation within the boundaries of the valley were over. Thutmose left his country, monarch of nearly all she surveyed. And, like it or not, the "vile" and "wretched" foreigner was now a part of Egyptian life. Cretans, Nubians, Syrians, Mitannians, Babylonians and Palestinians were now a familiar sight on the streets of Thebes. They came and went as merchants, traders, slaves, sightseers or bearers of tribute. The tradition-bound Egyptians grew used to these strangers but they never quite trusted or accepted them. The valley people continued to deride the foreigners' odd ways of life, their strange gods and—most of all—their inquiring and speculative habits of mind.

On a dark night in A.D. 1871, some 3,300 years after Thutmose the Third had died, three tomb robbers crept out of the Valley of the Kings. Walking single file, they started for home along a path that crossed the face of the cliff above Hatshepsut's temple of Deir el Bahri. All three men were weary and out of sorts. They had been digging

The eerie Valley of the Kings. Tourist roads now lead to the once-hidden underground tombs of the Pharaohs.

in the Valley of the Kings for months without making a single find.

Suddenly the leader of the band, an Arab named Abderrassul, stopped short in his tracks. A small black hole in the cliff face had caught his eye. Curious, he picked up a pebble and chucked it into the opening.

Then he and his companions stiffened. For they heard the pebble strike bottom with a faint hollow sound somewhere far down behind the face of the cliff. This sound meant only one thing to thieves as experienced as they. There was an ancient shaft behind the cliff face.

Forgetting their weariness, the three tomb robbers went at the little hole with their pickaxes. In a matter of moments it was large enough for Abderrassul to get his head and shoulders inside. Working swiftly, with great excitement, he tied one end of a coil of rope around his body and checked his matches and candles. Then he eased himself cautiously into the hole, feet first, and ordered his companions to lower him into the darkness. The long coil of rope was almost played out when a sharp tug signaled that Abderrassul had reached bottom.

Up on the cliff path, Abderrassul's brother and the third thief waited tensely. Not a sound reached them from below. Seconds stretched into minutes, minutes into a quarter-hour. Back in the desert a hyena wailed and chuckled. Bats swooped and circled through the night air. An owl hooted softly from Hatshepsut's ruined temple down below.

The two men eyed each other uneasily. Both knew that Meresger, snake goddess of the ancient Egyptians, lay coiled and ready to sink her deadly fangs into anyone who disturbed a Pharaoh's rest. And both had heard of the curse laid down by the ancient priests as they sealed the tombs of their god-kings: "I have set ablaze all the area around me; the flames will seize any man who approaches me with hostile intent. . . ."

What had happened to Abderrassul?

At this very moment, a bloodcurdling scream came from the bottom of the shaft, and the rope began to dance violently. The two thieves on the cliff path looked at each other wildly, and began hauling the rope upward with all their might.

Abderrassul's disheveled hair at last appeared in the opening. Then his wide, terror-filled eyes. And finally his smudged and sweat-streaked face. "Hurry!" he gasped as he tumbled out onto the path. "An *afrit*—an evil demon! There's an afrit down below!"

This was all that his superstitious companions needed to hear. Eyes starting from their sockets, they ran down the path as fast as they could go, with Abderrassul hard on their heels.

Back in the sleeping village, the three bid each other a shaky good night. Then Abderrassul and his brother hurried off to bed. Or so the third thief supposed.

Next morning, the story of the afrit at the bottom of the shaft was all over the village. A few days later, those who dared crept along the cliff path to the black hole. They soon came pelting back with news that a foul and evil smell—the sure sign of an afrit—was coming from the opening. From that day on, the villagers stayed well away from the cliff face and the hole where the evil demon dwelled.

And so time passed. Nearly ten years had gone by when the directors of the great museum down river in Cairo began receiving puzzling reports. Priceless Egyptian antiquities, never seen by the museum staff, were turning up in private collections in Europe and America. Since by law the museum had to pass on all ancient objects before they could be sold or exported, this could only mean that native thieves were at work. They must have found a hidden cache of valuable relics which they were selling off illegally, one by one.

The museum ordered a secret investigation. All evidence pointed to Thebes and, finally, to Abderrassul, who was arrested. Emile Brugsch, the museum's assistant curator, boarded the river steamer for Egypt's ancient capital. And there he listened in astonishment to the story Abderrassul had to tell.

When his companions had lowered him to the bottom of the cliff shaft ten years before, the tomb robber said, he had found himself in a narrow corridor. It was piled high with wooden coffins. Crawling over these, Abderrassul had followed the corridor to an underground burial chamber. There he had found even more coffins —Abderrassul could not say how many for his eyes were riveted on the chamber floor. It was ankle-deep in gold and silver and alabaster funerary equipment of all kinds.

Abderrassul had stared, stupefied, at the riches before him. His first impulse had been to race back to the shaft

A golden headdress—the kind of priceless treasure Abderrassul found at the bottom of the secret shaft behind the cliffs

and call his companions. But then he had hesitated. The friend who waited above with Abderrassul's brother was a good thief and a good companion. But he was not a blood relative. With fierce Arab loyalty, Abderrassul decided that his clan alone should benefit from this incredible find. And so he had seated himself on one of the ancient coffins, and tried to think of a way to keep these underground riches in the family. The afrit was his answer.

Later that night he had let his brother in on the secret. When they were sure that their friend, the third thief, was safely abed, the two men had crept out of their house. They had found and killed a donkey, dragged it back up the cliff path and heaved it down the shaft. In a few days, the donkey's decomposing body had given off an evil afrit smell. The villagers dared not explore the shaft. And for the next ten years, Abderrassul and his brother had safely plundered the underground chamber by night, quietly selling its treasures to tourists and black-market dealers.

Emile Brugsch of the Cairo Museum listened to this story with growing incredulity and excitement. Though it was July, and nearly 120 degrees in the shade, he went immediately to the shaft and had himself lowered. Like Abderrassul before him, Brugsch was stunned by what he saw. He crawled along the corridor into the underground chamber where, in his own words: ". . . Every inch . . . was covered with coffins and antiquities of all kinds. My astonishment was so overpowering that I scarcely knew whether I was awake or whether it was only a dream. . . . The further I advanced, the greater was the wealth displayed. . . ."

But it was the coffins more than the antiquities that excited Brugsch. Archaeologists had excavated tomb after tomb in the Valley of the Kings, only to find that they had been robbed of their royal mummies and funerary equipment long ago.

But here, before Brugsch's unbelieving eyes, were the mummies of thirty-six of the most famous kings and queens of ancient Egypt. Among them were Rameses the

Great; Pharaoh Ahmose, deliverer of Egypt from the Hyksos; Queen Ahmes, mother of Hatshepsut; Thutmose the First; Thutmose the Second; and—his mummy broken into three pieces—Pharaoh Thutmose the Third.

Ancient priests had removed these famous kings and queens from their tombs in the Valley of the Kings during a period of lawlessness late in Egypt's history. A series of bad floods had caused widespread famine and poverty, and thieves in numbers began despoiling the royal tombs. The ancient priests hastily ordered the shaft sunk behind the cliff above Deir el Bahri. When it was completed, they secretly reburied the kings and queens in simple wooden coffins, with as much of their funerary equipment as they were able to carry. Until Abderrassul and his companions had stumbled upon the entrance to the shaft, the royal mummies had lain undisturbed in their hiding place for some 3,000 years.

Brugsch ordered the underground chamber cleared. The royal mummies and their belongings were taken down river to the Cairo Museum. There, staff experts carefully put together the broken pieces of Thutmose the Third's body. And then, fascinated, they called their colleagues in to see.

The first great general in the history of the world had been barely five feet tall.

The Criminal of Akhetaton —Pharaoh Akhnaton

From about 1361 B.C. to about 1344 B.C.

Sixteen years after Abderrassul found his cache of royal treasures and mummies, a simple Arab peasant woman made an even more important archaeological find. Unlike Abderrassul, however, she did not stumble upon jewels and gold and silver. Her find looked so trashy and useless to her that she very nearly abandoned it to be drifted over by sand once again. If she had, archaeologists might still know almost nothing about a strange young man who turned out to be, some believe, the most fascinating Pharaoh of them all.

The peasant woman was a native of Tell el Amarna, a sleepy little village on the Nile about 250 miles down river from Thebes. On the day of her find she had gone back into the desert to dig for *sebakh*, a kind of nitrous soil used as fertilizer by the natives.

The woman had chosen a place at random and had started to work when her spade turned up several rectangular pieces of old clay. She tossed them aside impatiently, and went on digging. But, like the thieves who kept finding mummified crocodiles, she kept turning up spadeful after spadeful of the same crumbling pieces of clay.

Grumbling to herself, she decided to move on and try for sebakh in another spot. But as she bent down to pick up her gunny sack, she paused uncertainly. She had just noticed that the pieces of clay were covered with even lines of wedge-shaped markings.

Now the peasant woman of Tell el Amarna had no way of knowing that these wedge-shaped markings were Babylonian cuneiform. Or that Babylonian cuneiform was a form of writing used by the rulers of the ancient world in their letters to one another—letters written not on papyrus but on baked clay tablets.

All the Arab woman knew (or hoped) was that the wedge-shaped markings might mean that the old clay had some value. The foreigners who were digging all over Egypt often paid well for "junk" no better than this. On a gamble (and to the everlasting gratitude of archaeologists), the peasant woman packed the tablets —more than 350 of them—into her gunny sack and started back for the village.

There she had a stroke of great good luck. A neighbor bought the whole sackful of tablets from her for the princely sum of fifty cents. The woman hurried off with her riches. And that is the last that history knows of her.

The woman's neighbor now sold the tablets to a buyer who recognized the wedge-shaped markings for what they were. But cuneiform tablets had never before been found in Egypt. Experts disagreed on whether they were genuine or forged. The tablets passed from hand to hand until Sir Wallis Budge finally settled the matter.

Sir Wallis was a noted British archaeologist and cuneiform expert. When several of the clay pieces were brought to him for judgment, he studied them with growing excitement. The tablets were not forgeries. On the contrary, most of them were ancient and anguished cries for help from cities in Palestine and Syria to a Pharaoh about whom archaeologists knew almost nothing. The Tell el Amarna tablets, Budge announced, were "of very great historical importance."

And so, indeed, they were. For they opened the door on a little-known and extraordinary interlude in ancient Egyptian history—an interlude of about twenty-one years, known as the Amarna Heresy.

Four years after the peasant woman found the now-famous tablets, archaeologists began excavating in the empty desert behind Tell el Amarna. And little by little they uncovered not only the half-ruined palaces, temples and royal roadways of a great buried city; they also uncovered the story of a Pharaoh about whom they have been quarreling bitterly ever since.

The Pharaoh's name, for a time, was Amenhotep the Fourth. To some archaeologists he was "a fanatic," and "a madman." To others he was "a great reformer," "a saint" and "the most remarkable of all the Pharaohs . . . the first *individual* in human history."

Perhaps the Pharaoh of Tell el Amarna was all of these

Pharaoh Amenhotep the Third

things rolled into one, if that is possible. Certainly he was one of the most complex and extraordinary men in the history of the ancient world.

Some forty-five years after the death of Thutmose the Third, the Egyptian empire had reached new heights of power and wealth. Tribute and trade goods poured into Thebes from the far corners of the known world, and the valley people prospered as never before. The vassal states were so quiet that Pharaoh no longer had to march forth each spring to make a show of force in Syria, Palestine or Nubia. The ruling Pharaoh, Amenhotep the Third, had not left the valley for some ten or fifteen years. He devoted himself, instead, to vast building projects at home, and to living a life of such luxury and splendor that archaeologists have called him Amenhotep the Magnificent.

Thebes was now the major city of the ancient world—a great, sprawling, overcrowded metropolis. Thebans and foreigners elbowed their way through the city's almost impassable alleys. And underfoot everywhere—swelling the crowds and adding to the confusion—were Egyptian sightseers from all parts of the valley. They came with the hope of seeing Pharaoh, and to stare in awe at the monuments, temples and wide processional ways of their splendid, blazing capital. Most particularly they came to gape at Karnak. For Amon's temple precinct was now so huge that the three great modern cathedrals of St. Peter's in Rome, Notre Dame in Paris, and Milan in northern Italy could fit inside its encircling walls—with room to spare.

To escape the din and turmoil of the capital, Pharaoh Amenhotep the Third had built his Royal Precinct on the western bank of the Nile, across the river from the city. There, with his tiny, forceful wife, Queen Tiy, he lived a life as dazzling in its Oriental splendor as any tale from *The Arabian Nights' Entertainments*.

The court echoed to the sound of laughter and music,

day and night. Brilliantly dressed courtiers and foreign guests thronged the palace's flower-filled courtyards, its beautiful reception rooms and its columned banqueting halls. Days were given over to gossip and games, to picnicking on the river in gaily decorated barges, and to lion and antelope hunts in the desert behind the cliffs. When night fell, there were moonlight water festivals on the private lake Amenhotep had built for Queen Tiy near the palace. Or the King and Queen would feast until dawn with their guests, while jugglers, wrestlers and dancing girls entertained them to the music of flutes, oboes and harps.

Amenhotep and Tiy had several small daughters, but as yet no son. And so, rejoicing was valley-wide when the Queen—sometime around 1386 B.C.—gave birth to a boy. He was named Amenhotep, after his father.

Nothing at all is known about the childhood of Egypt's new Crown Prince—except that he was sickly from

Statuette of a lady of Amenhotep's court, wearing her perfume—a cone of scented ointment—atop her heavy black wig

birth. He apparently suffered from a glandular disorder that worsened as he grew older. But if young Amenhotep's adult interests and character are any indication, the future Pharaoh must have been a bookish and moody child. He would have been passionately interested in art, poetry and religion, and not the least interested in sports, military matters or the gay amusements of his father's court. His closest companion—if, indeed, he had any close companions—was almost certainly Nefertiti, his beautiful little cousin, or sister (archaeologists are not sure which).

As Amenhotep grew into his teens, he and Nefertiti became deeply involved in a battle that was taking place behind the scenes at court. For all was not as peaceful as it seemed in the Royal Precinct. Amenhotep's father and the High Priest of Amon were engaged in a silent struggle for power.

The great shadow of Karnak now stretched out across the land. Thutmose the Third's successors had continued to shower the King of the Gods with gifts of holdings throughout Egypt and the empire. By Amenhotep the Third's day, Karnak is believed to have owned more than one-third of all the arable land in the valley—as well as countless towns, fields and orchards in the vassal states. The revenues and tribute from these possessions flowed into Karnak in an ever-growing stream. The temple granaries, stockyards and warehouses were now almost as richly stocked as those in the Royal Precinct.

Karnak's enormous wealth gave the High Priest of Amon great political power, in addition to the power he held as the foremost religious leader in the land. And many in Pharaoh's court felt that the High Priest had grown dangerously ambitious. It was rumored that he sought to reduce Pharaoh to a figurehead and rule Egypt himself—not from the throne, but from the awesome regions of Karnak.

The idea of open warfare almost certainly never occurred to Amenhotep the Third—or to the High Priest. The positions of both men were unassailable. But tension between court and temple had steadily increased as the Crown Prince grew to manhood.

During these years, a new god called the Aton had risen to prominence at court. This new god was the sun itself. (*Aton* was an age-old Egyptian word for the actual physical orb of the sun. The great sun god Ra, for example, was said to live in the Aton.)

Worship of this new god, many archaeologists believe, was deliberately encouraged by Pharaoh as one means of undermining and curbing the High Priest's power. But there were other reasons, too, for the Aton's growing popularity at court.

As a result of the empire built by Thutmose the Third, many Egyptian nobles had married high-born ladies from Syria, Palestine, Babylonia and Mitanni. These foreign brides had taken easily to Egypt's ways, but less happily to her many strange gods. The Aton, however, was a deity they could understand and worship with a sense of familiarity and comfort. For the visible sun that rode high in the Egyptian sky was the very same sun that warmed the mountains and valleys of their native lands.

The ladies of Pharaoh's cosmopolitan court took the Aton to their hearts.

There was also another reason for the growth of the Aton cult at court. Egypt's empire was now enormous. A *universal* god, a god that could be understood and worshiped in common by the diverse peoples of the vassal states, would act as a strong, unifying force, tending to hold the sprawling empire together. The Aton, visible and understandable to all, perfectly answered the need for such a universal god.

For these various reasons, then, Amenhotep the Third had built an Aton temple within the Royal Precinct. There he and his court paid homage to the visible sun, despite the tight-lipped disapproval of the High Priest of Amon. Pharaoh also built a small Aton temple in Thebes, just east of the towering walls of Karnak. But there was no open break with the priests of Amon. Amenhotep also continued to worship at Karnak, as his royal forefathers had always done before him.

No one can say how sincerely Pharaoh believed in the Aton. But there can be little doubt about the feelings of his son, the Crown Prince. As he grew to manhood, young Amenhotep became a passionate devotee of the Aton—and an implacable foe of Amon and his priesthood.

When the Crown Prince was about twenty-one years old, he and the lovely Nefertiti were married. Three years later, the now ill and aging Amenhotep the Third named his son co-regent of Egypt. In a great coronation ceremony at Hermonthis near Thebes, the young prince was crowned Amenhotep the Fourth.

The new Pharaoh and his Queen made an odd and unlikely couple. For Nefertiti was as slim and beautiful as her husband was ungainly and misshapen. His illness had by now distorted the young Pharaoh's body. His hips were heavy, his stomach bloated and his shoulders sloping. His face—dominated by dark, intense eyes—was as narrow as a hatchet blade. But in spite of his appearance, Amenhotep seems to have had great personal charm—when he chose to use it. Certainly there was no doubt about Nefertiti's devotion to him. It was clear for all to see.

When the long coronation ceremony had come to an end, the new Pharaoh and his Queen returned to the royal palace. And Egypt, the festivities over, went on about her business. For a time, apparently, all went on as usual. Amenhotep the Fourth conducted himself as tradition demanded. He met with his counselors, consulted the High Priest of Amon on state matters and worshiped regularly at Karnak. It went almost unnoticed, except by the priests of Amon, that during this time Pharaoh began to enlarge and beautify the Aton temple in Thebes.

Then, without warning, Amenhotep declared open warfare on Amon. Sometime during the second or third year of his reign, he issued a terse decree from the palace. The name of the district in Thebes where the Aton temple was located was to be changed to "The Brightness of Aton the Great." And Thebes itself, the City of

Amon, was to be renamed "The City of the Brightness of Aton."

A short while later, the Great Royal Barge, with Amenhotep aboard, put out from the Theban waterfront and headed down river.

When Pharaoh returned to the capital about ten days later, he shut himself away in the palace with his royal architects and engineers. Soon thereafter, boatload after boatload of stone masons, carpenters, sculptors and gardeners left the docks of Thebes.

In a matter of days the bewildered capital learned where the ships had gone. Pharaoh was building a great new city down river. He could no longer tolerate Thebes, dominated as it was by Amon and his huge temple. Amenhotep's new city was to be dedicated to the Aton, and the Aton alone.

Pharaoh had found the site himself on his trip down river. Located some 250 miles below Thebes, it was an 8-mile stretch of empty desert, completely enclosed by the valley cliffs. The cliffs came forward to the river at the lower end of the site, swept back in a wide semicircle and then came forward to the river again at the site's upper end. Here, in this protected and isolated spot, Amenhotep began the building of Akhetaton—his "City of the Horizon."

He drew up the plans himself—or so it is believed. And since he had the entire labor force of Egypt at his command, the city seemed to grow almost overnight. "White and fair," it contained a vast royal palace, spacious residences for Pharaoh's nobles, studios for the royal artists, a workmen's village, governmental offices and a police barracks. The city's wide streets were bordered with shade trees imported from Asia, and everywhere there were ornamental pools, pleasure gardens and a profusion of flowers. Dominating the whole was the enormous temple to Pharaoh's god. It bore no resemblance at all to Karnak, with its awesome gloom and dark Holy of Holies. The Aton temple in the new city blazed with light, standing roofless and open to the sun in the once-barren desert.

As the new city neared completion, Pharaoh one day abruptly announced that he was changing his name. He was no longer to be called Amenhotep, meaning "Amon Is Satisfied." Henceforth he was to be known as Akhnaton—"He Who Is Beneficial to Aton."

It was the death knell of the god Amon. Pharaoh's name had great significance in ancient Egypt, for it often indicated state policy in religious matters. By changing his name to Akhnaton, the king was notifying Egypt and the empire that the Aton had replaced Amon as the crown-supported first god of Egypt.

But this was not all. Pharaoh next ordered the Amon priesthood disbanded. Karnak was to be closed. The temple holdings and revenues were to revert to the crown. And Amon's name was to be erased from all the monuments, temples, steles and statues where it appeared. The former King of the Gods was to be utterly banished from the minds and memories of the valley people.

Last of all, Akhnaton announced to the stunned Thebans that he was abandoning their city. The City of the Horizon had not been built as a religious center alone. It was to serve as the new capital of Egypt.

Not long thereafter, a great flotilla of ships pulled away from the stone wharfs of Thebes and moved off down river. The Great Royal Barge took the lead with Pharaoh, Nefertiti and their two little daughters aboard. With them were two of Akhnaton's most trusted counselors —Chief Adviser Ay (thought to be Queen Tiy's brother) and the young and handsome Haremhab, commander of the Egyptian armies.

Behind Pharaoh's ship came barge after barge filled with Akhnaton's supporters, their families, servants and household possessions. Some of these courtiers may have genuinely believed in the Aton, as Pharaoh did. Others may have pretended belief because it was to their advantage to do so. And still others may have followed the young Pharaoh because they would have found it unthinkable to oppose their god-king in any matter at all.

Whatever their reasons, all of the courtiers had given up much in leaving Thebes. They had abandoned their estates, the tombs they were building for themselves in the western cliffs, and a familiar, gay and ordered way of life. But Pharaoh had offered each of his followers a new estate in Akhetaton. And he had promised each the gift of a new tomb in the cliffs that ringed the City of the Horizon.

History does not record what Queen Tiy and her invalid husband, Amenhotep the Third, thought of their son's action. They did not move to the new city, but stayed on in the half-empty palace beneath the western cliffs. With them remained their personal retinues and those nobles—no one knows how many—who feared Akhnaton's revolutionary defiance of Amon, and could not bring themselves to break completely with everything they had believed in and lived for all their lives.

The removal of the court cast a blight over Thebes. Its great stone wharfs lay virtually deserted under the hot sun, as tribute and trade goods went to the new docks down river. Bleakest of all was Karnak. Weeds soon filled the temple courtyards, and stray dogs scavenged among its towering forest of columns. But there was a rumor abroad that Karnak was not as deserted as it seemed. The High Priest of Amon and his disbanded brotherhood were said to meet regularly in the underground recesses of the temple, to plot the overthrow of the heretic Pharaoh—or even, some said, to do away with him altogether.

Pharaoh Akhnaton could have relieved the economic distress in Thebes had he chosen to do so. But once settled in his new city, he seemed to turn his back on Egypt and the rest of the world. Delegating governmental matters to his counselors, he devoted himself almost entirely to his family, his city and his god.

Life in flower-filled Akhetaton must have had the unreal quality of a dream. Days revolved around worship of the Aton. The rituals were simple, and without mystery. No image of the god was hidden away, to be

This limestone relief, uncovered at Tell el Amarna, shows the Pharaoh Akhnaton and his Queen worshiping the Aton. The Aton is represented by a sun disk.

bathed, anointed, dressed and fed each day. There were no statues or images of the Aton at all. The god was merely symbolized by a painting or carving of the sun, from which rays descended earthward, each ray ending in a hand or an *ankh*, the Egyptian symbol of life.

Nor did any pageantry and display surround the Aton ceremonials. At sunrise, the royal family and court gathered in the great open courtyard of the temple. A choir sang and harpists played. Then, as the Aton rose above the eastern cliffs, a simple offering of fruits and flowers was placed upon the high altar. At high noon, when the Aton blazed down from directly overhead, there was a second ceremony of offerings and songs. And, with Nefertiti presiding, there was a third ceremony at sunset, as Pharaoh's god sank out of sight behind the western cliffs.

During his first year in Akhetaton, Pharaoh was often seen in public during the hours between religious services. With Nefertiti and one or another of his little daughters (he had six altogether), Akhnaton would drive out in his chariot to oversee progress on the city's many uncompleted buildings. Sometimes the royal couple sped along the Great Royal Roadway to the north end of the city, where Akhnaton was building a second palace, complete with private zoo and aviary. Another day, they would gallop back in the desert to inspect the tombs Pharaoh was building for his favorite nobles in the cliffs. Or, again, they would make their way up a desolate, scorpion-infested ravine between the cliffs to the lonely spot where Akhnaton was building a tomb for himself and his family.

And scarcely a day passed that Pharaoh did not visit the studios of his painters and sculptors. For Akhnaton himself, according to his Chief Sculptor Bek, had taught his artists a revolutionary new way of painting.

From childhood, Akhnaton must have fretted against the age-old traditions of Egyptian art. Animals and birds were painted and sculpted in a lifelike manner—in flight or on the run. But since the days of unification, 1,800 years before, strict artistic and religious rules had governed the drawing of human beings. Each part of the body was shown in what the Egyptians considered its most typical pose—head in profile, shoulders and hips facing forward and legs in profile. As a result, the portrayal of people was so rigid and unchanging that it was hard to tell a painting made in Akhnaton's day from one made when Cheops ruled, 1,500 years earlier.

The rules governing the painting or sculpting of Pharaoh were particularly strict. As a great god, he must always be shown larger than lifesize, towering over the little mortals he governed. He was to be painted only in one of several standard poses. And he must always be shown as young, slim and handsome—no matter how old, fat and ugly he might actually be.

Akhnaton changed all these rules. He trained his artists in a rudimentary use of perspective. And he insisted that they paint and sculpt people as they were. Not only was Akhnaton's oddly shaped body to be

A limestone relief of Nefertiti and Akhnaton in which the sculptor has faithfully reproduced the Pharaoh's heavy hips and bloated stomach in the manner requested by the Pharaoh himself

faithfully reproduced, but the standard Pharaonic poses were to be banished. Pharaoh and the royal family were to be painted and sculpted as they were, and as they went about their daily tasks and pleasures.

As a result, the artists of the new city portrayed Akhnaton holding audience—with one arm around Nefertiti's waist. They showed him lounging in his garden, dandling one of his little daughters on his knee, or gnawing away at the leg of a roast duck at dinner. All of Egypt could now see their awesome god-king in intimate, homey little scenes such as these. They made for a refreshing and naturalistic form of art. But in tradition-bound and tradition-loving Egypt, that may well have been a grave political mistake. The Egyptian people wanted, and needed, to think of their god-king as awesome, remote, all-powerful. Akhnaton's art may have seriously diminished his stature in his people's eyes—and even caused them to ridicule him slyly behind his back.

After his second or third year in Akhetaton, Pharaoh was seen less often about the city. His health had worsened. But, more importantly, he had by now become totally obsessed with the deeper meaning of his god. At last he wrote a hymn to the Aton that expressed everything he had come to believe:

Thou risest beautifully in the horizon of heaven,
O living Aton who creates Life!
When thou risest in the eastern horizon
Thou fillest every land with thy beauty . . .
Thy rays, they embrace the lands to the limits of all thou hast made . . .
How manifold are thy works!
They are hidden from the face of men, O sole god . . .
Thou madest the earth at thy will when thou wast alone—
Men, cattle, all animals, everything on earth that goes on its feet,

Everything that is on high that flies with its wings . . .
Thy rays nourish every field.
When thou risest, they live and flourish for thee.
Thou makest the seasons . . .
Thou hast made heaven afar off in order to shine therein
And to see all thou hast made, thou alone. . . .

Long before the ancient world was ready or able to accept such a concept, Akhnaton had reached the conclusion that there was one god, and one god alone, in all the universe.

If there was but one true god, Akhnaton reasoned, then all the hundreds and hundreds of Egyptian and foreign gods signified nothing and must be swept away. Having reached this conclusion, Pharaoh acted upon it with the abruptness and indifference to consequences that characterized every move he made. From the City of the Horizon a decree went forth to all Egypt, forbidding worship of any god save the Aton. Osiris, Ra and all the other age-old deities so beloved by the valley people were to be banished from the world forever.

When the decree was issued, there were stirrings of alarm, even among Akhnaton's devoted followers in the new city. And the rest of the country must have been appalled. The lives of the valley people were sufficiently awry by this time, anyway. Pharaoh had been so absorbed by the Aton, and so lax in his overlordship of the country, that Egypt was once again "topsy-turvy." Disorder and lawlessness were not so rampant as they had been in the valley's Dark Ages, so long before. But unemployed soldiers roamed the land, plundering and robbing as they saw fit. Tax collectors, with no strong central authority to control them, were dunning the people unfairly. And everywhere the unfrocked priests of Amon wandered the byways, secretly stirring up trouble against the "heretic" who sat on the throne of Egypt.

Now, to deepen the valley's distress, came Akhnaton's order banishing the gods whom the Egyptians had loved, feared and prayed to for more than 2,000 years—the gods who guided and controlled every moment of their lives. The valley people's fear and dismay can only be imagined. But once they had recovered from their first shock, there is every indication that they dared to ignore Pharaoh's order. They went on worshiping their familiar gods, but in secret. They would have been encouraged to do so—not only by the priests of Amon, but by the priests of all the other gods that Pharaoh now sought to overthrow.

Even the people in Pharaoh's own City of the Horizon took the great risk of defying his order. When archaeologists excavated the workmen's village there, they found dozens and dozens of small household statuettes of Egypt's familiar gods. They had been kept hidden, and had been prayed to in secret, almost within sight of the royal palace.

Now trouble arose from a different quarter. Beyond Egypt's borders, her great empire was beginning to disintegrate.

The mighty army of Egypt had not been seen in the

vassal states for more than twenty years. As a result, many of the north Syrian princes were beginning to agitate secretly for freedom from Egypt's overlordship.

Boldest among these princes were Aziru and his son Abdashirta, rulers in Pharaoh's name of a city-state in the Orontes River Valley. These two plotters had found a ready ally against Egypt in the wily old King of the Hittites, a powerful people who lived in central Turkey. With Hittite support, Aziru and his son were now marching against Pharaoh's north Syrian possessions, taking town after town and throwing the northern empire into turmoil. In addition, a nomadic desert people called the Habiru were attacking the Egyptian vassal cities in Palestine.

From these beleaguered northern cities, courier after courier galloped down the dusty roads into Egypt, bearing desperate letters to Pharaoh from his Syrian and Palestinian administrators.

"I need men to save the rebellion of this land," wrote one governor. "Give me soldiers. . . ."

"Abdashirta is marching with his brethren," cried out another. "March against him and smite him! . . . The land is the King's land; and since I have talked thus and you have not moved, the city of Simyra has been lost. There is no money to buy horses; all is finished . . . give me thirty companies of horse with chariots, men, men. . . ."

And from Palestine: "All the lands of the King have broken away. . . . The Habiru are plundering all the lands of the King. If no troops come in this very year, then all of the lands of the King are lost. . . ."

Did Akhnaton ever see these desperate appeals for help? Some archaeologists think not. There is a suggestion that Pharaoh's foreign minister was in league with the traitorous Aziru, and simply filed the letters away without showing them to Akhnaton.

More probably, Pharaoh did see the letters, and ignored them. There was no place in his religious philosophy for war and violence. The Aton loved all men equally. Pharaoh's god was a god of peace.

In any case, whether he saw the letters or not, Pharaoh took no action. Neither armies nor funds were sent to put down the rebellions in the north. The poignant appeals for help were filed away in the Foreign Office. And there they lay during the long, long centuries until the peasant woman of Tell el Amarna dug them up out of the sand again, some 3,000 years later.

Akhnaton's invalid father, Amenhotep the Third, had by this time died in his palace up river at Thebes. And after a suitable period of mourning, Queen Mother Tiy prepared to visit her son.

During the years that Akhnaton had lived in the City of the Horizon, Tiy must have been dismayed and then angered by her son's conduct. For the Queen Mother had watched Egypt sinking deeper and deeper into disorder from lack of leadership on Pharaoh's part. Now she was forced to stand helplessly by as the empire fell apart—and as her son did nothing.

Both Haremhab, commander of the army, and Chief

Queen Tiy

Adviser Ay, Akhnaton's elderly counselor, had probably journeyed up river more than once, to confer secretly with Tiy. Neither man, it is believed, could any longer reach Akhnaton (some say Pharaoh's illness had by now affected his mind). Both Haremhab and Ay were undoubtedly as alarmed as Tiy about the perilous state of Egypt and the empire. The two may have pleaded with the Queen Mother to intercede with her son. Or Tiy, quite independently, may have decided that the time had come to take matters into her own hands.

Whatever the case, the Queen Mother now dressed herself in her most impressive regal robes and voyaged in state down river. Akhnaton, Nefertiti and their six little daughters were at the wharf of the new city to greet her. The royal family proceeded in state through the festive and welcoming city. Then they retired to the private apartments of the royal palace.

And now a veil of mystery falls over the happenings in the City of the Horizon. The end of Akhnaton's story is filled with uncertainties. But from the few facts at their command, archaeologists have pieced it together as best they can. They believe that Tiy closeted herself with her son soon after her arrival in Akhetaton. In a series of stormy interviews, the Queen Mother must have forcefully brought home to Akhnaton just how matters stood at home and abroad. And she must have insisted that he face up to the fact that the Aton had utterly failed to capture the minds and hearts of the valley people. They wanted the freedom to worship their old gods openly once again. And they wanted once again to bow down before Amon—the great god who had won them an empire once, and could win it for them again. If order was to be restored to the Egyptian world, Karnak must be reopened at once. Akhnaton must be reconciled with the High Priest of Amon and restore him to his former power.

The argument must have raged for days. In the end, Tiy won. Akhnaton was surely most seriously ill by now: the spirit and fight had gone out of him. Nefertiti (archaeologists do not know why) fell into disgrace soon after Tiy's victory. Perhaps because she refused to abandon the Aton, Nefertiti was banished from the palace and sent to live in exile in the North Palace of

Akhetaton. With her went her personal servants and Akhnaton's half-brother, a little boy of about six named Tutankhaton.

Tutankhaton had an older brother named Smenkhkare, who now married Akhnaton's eldest daughter. Smenkhkare was named co-ruler of Egypt by the ailing Pharaoh and sent up river to Thebes with his new bride. There they were to reopen Karnak and restore the High Priest of Amon to his former position.

Three years later both Smenkhkare and his wife were dead—from what causes, or by whose hand, no one knows. And at almost the same time, down river in the City of the Horizon, Pharaoh Akhnaton, too, died—presumably from natural causes but almost certainly in great weariness of spirit. He was no more than forty-two years of age.

Egypt was now without a Pharaoh, and Nefertiti is thought to have acted swiftly—perhaps in a last attempt to keep Atonism alive. Hastily she married little Tutankhaton to her twelve-year-old daughter, Ankhsenpaaton, who was now heiress to the throne. Nine-year-old Tutankhaton, who had been raised in the Aton faith, thus became the new Pharaoh of Egypt.

For a time, Tutankhaton ruled from the City of the Horizon. But then he was brought back to Thebes by the now reinstated and triumphant priests of Amon. They forced him to change his name from Tutankh*aton* to Tutankh*amon*. And for the rest of his short life—he died when he was eighteen—he ruled Egypt as a puppet of

The gold-and-enamel death mask that covered the shrunken, mummified face of Pharaoh Tutankhamon

the High Priest. Amon was once more King of the Gods, and his priests were more powerful than ever before. They were to hold and increase this power for the balance of ancient Egypt's history.

When Tutankhamon died, Chief Adviser Ay (now a very old man indeed) ruled as Pharaoh for about five years. Then he too died, and Haremhab, Akhnaton's commander of the armies, seized the throne. As Pharaoh, Haremhab devoted his long reign to restoring order in the valley and to firmly leading Egypt back into the age-old ways of her forefathers.

It was under Haremhab that persecution of Akhnaton's memory began. The priests of Amon now turned against the dead Pharaoh, as he had once turned against them. Akhnaton's name was erased wherever it appeared on monuments, temples or steles. And when he was referred to at all, it was always as "that criminal of Akhetaton."

Akhnaton's court, sensing the way the wind was blowing, had quietly begun to desert the City of the Horizon before Pharaoh had died. One by one, his nobles and favorites had closed their houses and sailed back to Thebes, to return to Akhetaton no more. With Akhnaton's death and the removal of Tutankhamon to Thebes, the City of the Horizon gradually became a ghost town. The insidious desert sands began drifting in over the streets and gardens and the great courtyard of Aton's temple. Jackals from the high desert prowled the once-splendid Royal Roadway by night. Scorpions scrabbled along the palace corridors, and owls and bats inhabited the dark and desolate reception halls.

Before many years had passed, the City of the Horizon had half-disappeared beneath the encroaching desert. Soon it had vanished altogether. And with it vanished all memory of the god who Akhnaton had prayed would live on.

"Till the swan be black and the raven white, till the mountains rise up and move away and water flows uphill . . ."

On November 26, 1922, a small group of men and women stood before a sealed doorway at the end of an underground passage in the Valley of the Kings.

A small opening had been made in the upper left-hand corner of the stone door. In front of it, a candle in one hand and an iron testing rod in the other, stood an archaeologist named Howard Carter. Directly behind him was the English Lord Carnarvon, who had financed Carter's excavations in the desolate burying ground of Egypt's ancient Pharaohs. Behind Carnarvon, in a tense little group, stood Lady Carnarvon and some of the most noted Egyptologists of the day. They had all hurried there, some from as far away as London, in response to a cable from Carter to Lord Carnarvon. It read: "At last have made wonderful discovery in Valley; a magnificent tomb with seals intact. . . ."

It was the words "with seals intact" that had brought these noted people to Thebes on the double. For though tomb after tomb had been found in the valley, all had been entered and robbed in antiquity. Carter's cable implied that he had discovered a tomb untouched since ancient priests had sealed up its entrance thousands of years before.

Had Carter actually found such a tomb? Let him tell in his own words what happened that day in 1922, as he stood before the underground doorway. With hands that

Deep under the ground, archaeologists peer into one of the golden shrines in Tutankhamon's tomb.

"trembled," Howard Carter carefully inserted the testing rod into the hole he had made in the door. As he later wrote:

> Darkness and blank space, as far as an iron testing rod could reach, showed that whatever lay beyond was empty. Candle tests were applied as a precaution against possible foul gases, and then, widening the hole a little, I inserted the candle and peered in, Lord Carnarvon . . . standing anxiously beside me to hear the verdict. At first I could see nothing, the hot air escaping from the chamber causing the candle flame to flicker, but presently, as my eyes grew accustomed to the light, details of the room within emerged slowly from the mist, strange animals, statues, and gold —everywhere the glint of gold. For the moment—an eternity it must have seemed to the others standing by—I was struck dumb with amazement, and when Lord Carnarvon, unable to stand the suspense any longer, inquired anxiously, "Can you see anything?" it was all I could do to get out the words, "Yes, wonderful things." . . .

Carter had seen wonderful things indeed. Piled on top of each other and filling every inch of space beyond the door were golden couches, dismantled gold chariots, life-size statues wearing gold kilts and gold sandals, inlaid caskets, beds, intricately carved chairs, bouquets of flowers, a great golden throne. . . .

> Surely never before in the whole history of excavation [Carter continued] had such an amazing sight been seen as the light of our torch revealed to us . . . the first light that had pierced the darkness of the chamber for three thousand years. . . .
>
> Presently it dawned upon our bewildered brains that in

all this medley of objects before us, there was no coffin or trace of mummy. [Carter swung the torch around the room again and for the first time noticed a door in the opposite wall.]

The explanation gradually dawned upon us. We were but on the threshold of our discovery. What we saw was merely an antechamber. Behind the . . . door there were to be other chambers, possibly a succession of them, and in one of them, beyond any shadow of a doubt, in all his magnificent panoply of death, we should find the Pharaoh lying.

Carter was right. When the far door was at last opened, the archaeologist found an enormous golden shrine. Within it was a series of smaller shrines and within these a series of coffins, the innermost made of solid gold. When its heavy lid was lifted free, there lay the mummy of Akhnaton's half-brother, the boy-Pharaoh Tutankhamon.

Over his face was a portrait death mask in solid gold. His hands and toenails were sheathed in gold. There were jeweled necklaces about his throat, and gold rings on his fingers. . . .

It was a stupendous find, one of the greatest in the history of Egyptology. But, once they had recovered from their wonder and excitement, the discovery set archaeologists to musing. For Tutankhamon had been one of the least important of the Pharaohs of ancient Egypt. Yet his tomb had been filled with a profusion of incredible and priceless objects. What marvels, archaeologists wondered, would the tombs of such mighty Pharaohs as Cheops and Thutmose the Third have

Beneath the brilliant wall frescoes of his tomb, the mummy of Tutankhamon lies within an outer casing of gold.

contained—had excavators been lucky enough to find them unopened?

Archaeologists have never found the mummies of Akhnaton and Nefertiti. When the heretic Pharaoh's tomb behind the cliffs at Tell el Amarna was opened, one of the archaeologists present reported finding the body of a man that had been burned shortly after mummification. The priests of Amon may well have burned Akhnaton's body after entombment (if this mummy was actually his). For in no more ruthless way could they have taken vengeance upon the Pharaoh they so detested. By destroying his earthly body, the Amon priests would have condemned Akhnaton's spirit, or ka, to wander the deserts as a lonely ghost, for the rest of time.

The Beginning of the End —Pharaoh Rameses the Second

From about 1291 B.C. to about 1224 B.C.

With Pharaoh Haremhab's death, the long and brilliant Eighteenth Dynasty came to an end. After the turbulent years under Akhnaton, Egypt had returned to her old ways, her old art forms and her old gods. Akhnaton and his Aton were all but forgotten —though the valley people still superstitiously averted their eyes as they passed the crumbling City of the Horizon on their way up or down river.

Haremhab died without heirs and the throne passed to his vizier, Rameses, the first Pharaoh of the Nineteenth Dynasty. He and his son, Seti, devoted themselves primarily to valley affairs. And it was not until Seti's son, Rameses the Second, mounted the throne that Egypt once again turned her eyes seriously toward empire.

Rameses the Second was crowned Pharaoh in about

1291 B.C. He was eighteen years old, and looked every inch a god-king. Tall for an Egyptian, he was handsome, slim and athletic. (His father, by all accounts, had made him run two miles before breakfast every morning.)

Right after his coronation, Rameses journeyed up river beyond the First Cataract to Abu Simbel, where he was later to build one of the most famous temples in Egypt. From Abu Simbel, he came down the Nile on the rising flood as though he himself were bringing the swollen life-giving waters to his people. Rameses paid his respects to the High Priest of Amon at Thebes. And from there, he proceeded slowly down river to the Delta, showing himself majestically to his people on the way.

And then Pharaoh prepared to reconquer Egypt's vast empire, so sadly disintegrated under Akhnaton's rule. Nubia was still under Egyptian control, but the Hittites had by this time taken most of north Syria, and were penetrating southward into Palestine.

During the first four years of his reign, Rameses campaigned along the eastern shores of the Mediterranean, retaking the coastal cities so necessary to him as bases. And for four years the wily Hittites watched him, and waited. Then they pounced.

As Rameses was mapping out his fifth year's campaign, couriers from the north stumbled into Pharaoh's court with alarming news. Mutuwallis, king of the Hittites, had gathered together a vast army of allies. He was now marching south toward the Syrian city of Kadesh, preparing to take Egypt's remaining vassal states away from her. The enemy, said the couriers, numbered

One of the many enormous statues of Pharaoh Rameses the Second that fill the interior of his temple at Abu Simbel

at least thirty thousand and "filled the whole land, covering the hills and valleys, like locusts . . ."

Rameses did not hesitate. His army was ready and waiting—a force of twenty thousand soldiers and charioteers. They were divided into four divisions of five thousand men each, and marched under the standards of Egypt's four greatest gods—Amon, Ra, Ptah and Sutekh.

At the head of the Division of Amon, and with his tame lion loping along beside his chariot, Rameses marched out of Egypt on to the great coastal road leading north—the road Thutmose the Third had taken some two hundred years earlier.

Twenty-nine days after he left the Egyptian frontier, Pharaoh reached the heights overlooking the valley of Kadesh. Below him lay a wide plain, divided from north to south by the river Orontes. The city of Kadesh was just visible in the distance, some ten miles up the valley. There was no sign of an enemy encampment beneath its walls. And the valley itself lay quiet and still in the late-afternoon sunlight. There was not a Hittite soldier in sight.

Rameses was not surprised. For days his advance scouts had reported no sign of the enemy. In their opinion, Mutuwallis and his forces were still far to the north.

In perfect confidence Rameses camped in the mountains that night and the next morning descended onto the plain. As he was about to ford the river, two Hittite deserters were brought before him. Mutuwallis, they said, had been in the valley not long before. But he had fled north at news of Pharaoh's coming. The enemy king was now "sitting" in the distant city of Aleppo, too frightened to engage the mighty army of Egypt.

Pleased and flattered with this news, Rameses decided to take the undefended city of Kadesh before moving north. Fording the river, he set out up the valley with his personal bodyguard and the Division of Amon. The

Division of Ra, well to the rear, was just coming down from the heights. The other two divisions had not yet left camp.

Rameses marched along with no sense of impending danger. The sun shone brightly, the river sparkled and the balmy air was full of the sounds and smells of spring. There was no one to be seen in the quiet valley and Rameses had no reason to suspect that he was walking straight into a trap.

At midday Pharaoh arrived beneath the forbidding walls and barred gates of Kadesh. He ordered his troops to make camp, and summoned his officers and scouts for a conference. And then disaster struck.

The Hittite "deserters" at the river crossing had actually been spies, sent to deceive Rameses about the enemy's whereabouts. Mutuwallis was not "sitting" in distant Aleppo at all. He and his army of thirty thousand were hiding on the other side of Kadesh. And now, with the shock of a thunderclap, the Hittite chariotry broke from behind the city walls. Ignoring Rameses for the moment, they galloped down the valley to cut off the Division of Ra, which was coming up some two miles back. Caught completely off guard, half the Ra Division retreated in disorder. The other half fled desperately up the valley to Pharaoh's camp, the Hittite charioteers hard on their heels. In their panic, the remnants of the Ra Division surged straight through camp and beyond, carrying most of the bewildered and terror-stricken Division of Amon with them.

Rameses, as he later told the story, was left alone to

face 2,500 Hittite charioteers, with only his personal bodyguard to help him.

As the enemy closed in around him, Pharaoh managed to send off a message to the Divisions of Ptah and Sutekh, ordering them to advance to his aid with all speed. Then he turned to face the Hittites. Leaping into his chariot, he tied the reins around his waist to leave his hands free. He lifted up his head, sent forth a great cry for help to Amon in distant Thebes—and charged.

The ring of chariots around Pharaoh was weakest along the river bank. And it was here that Rameses attacked. Six times he hurled his chariot against the Hittites—so successfully that he drove them into the river, "like crocodiles."

King Mutuwallis, in the meantime, had come out from behind Kadesh with a force of eight thousand infantrymen. He stood watching the fight from the opposite bank of the Orontes River. The river, according to Rameses, was now churning with thrashing horses and drowning men. And King Mutuwallis stood, "averted, shrinking and afraid" at the sight. Turning to fight the other Hittite charioteers, Rameses found his arm so strengthened by Amon that "The 2,500 spans of chariotry, in whose midst I was, [became] heaps of corpses before my horses."

Be that as it may, the unequal contest could not go on. Rameses was caught in a desperate trap. And he would have been captured or killed in a matter of moments, had it not been for three unexpected developments.

First, the fleeing divisions of Amon and Ra had

abandoned Pharaoh's camp with its stacked armaments, its tethered horses, its unhitched golden chariots, its royal pavilion—and Rameses' golden throne. At sight of all this booty, most of the Hittite charioteers wheeled away from Rameses, leaped to the ground and fell to looting.

Second, a contingent of Egyptian allies arrived unexpectedly on the scene, having come inland from the coast to rendezvous with Pharaoh in the valley. They flung themselves on the looting Hittites. And they were soon joined by the soldiers of Amon and Ra, who had recovered from their panic and returned to the fight.

Third, for some inexplicable reason King Mutuwallis did not throw his eight thousand infantry into the battle. He and his soldiers remained where they were during the entire struggle—watching as spectators from the other side of the river.

The battle raged on during the long afternoon. Then, toward sunset, the standard of the Division of Ptah was seen through the dust and confusion. This division, its soldiers rested and fresh, turned the tide of the battle. Not long after they arrived on the scene, the Hittite chariotry fled in disorder and Mutuwallis retreated to safety within the walls of Kadesh.

Rameses did not wait to lay siege to the city, or to face Mutuwallis in battle again. Gathering together the remnants of his four divisions, he turned tail and retreated to Egypt.

Once back in the Nile Valley, Rameses claimed for himself a stupendous victory against the enemy. "While he was alone, having no army with him," Pharaoh said, "he had repelled all lands through terror of him, so that all foreign countries were giving praise to his goodly countenance."

But in truth the Battle of Kadesh was no victory at all. Rameses had walked into a trap, had lost great numbers of his army, had failed to capture Kadesh—and had neither defeated the Hittites decisively, nor driven them north into their own lands again. And yet, as Egyptologist John Wilson said, "There is no episode in Egyptian history that occupies so much carved wall space in Egyptian temples" as Rameses' account of his great personal triumph in the Battle of Kadesh.

In fact, when archaeologists first started to work in Egypt, they not only found Rameses' account of the battle depicted on temple walls up and down the valley. They also, it seemed to them, found his name carved on most of the monuments, steles and obelisks in the land. Concluding that Rameses must have been the mightiest of ancient Egypt's Pharaohs, the archaeologists named him Rameses the Great. Later, they somewhat sheepishly revised their opinion. For they discovered that Rameses had gone up and down the Nile, appropriating the monuments of his predecessors and carving his name over theirs. Rameses was not so much a mighty Pharaoh as a mighty egoist and self-publicizer.

After the Battle of Kadesh, Rameses continued to campaign each year against the Hittites in Syria and Palestine. Towns were captured by the Egyptians, recaptured by the Hittites and taken again by the Egyptians.

Rameses "smiting" the Asiatics. This is one of the many portrayals of the Pharaoh's battle with the Hittites that appear on temple walls up and down the Nile Valley.

Over the years, the two armies fought each other to a standstill. At last, weary of the long-drawn-out conflict, the warring nations signed a treaty of peace.

The pact was never broken. Its continuing success was celebrated sixteen years later by a great state marriage between Rameses and the daughter of the Hittite king. The little princess made her way down into Egypt with a vast retinue of courtiers, ladies-in-waiting and soldiers. They were followed by strings of fine horses, herds of cattle and cartloads of gold and silver—her dowry for her future husband. Pharaoh sent an imposing escort to meet his bride. And, as it was recorded at the time, "The daughter of the Great Prince of Hatti marched to Egypt, while the infantry, chariotry and officials of His Majesty accompanied her, mingling with the infantry and chariotry of Hatti. . . . They ate and drank together, being of one heart like brothers, for peace and brotherhood were between them. . . ."

Pharaoh awaited the Princess in his pillared throne room. When she was at last brought before him, he "saw that she was fair of face [like] a goddess . . . she was beautiful in the heart of His Majesty, and he loved her more than anything."

Pharaoh's little Hittite bride was not his only wife. Rameses outlived seven Great Royal Wives and an untold number of secondary wives and concubines. By them all he had at least one hundred sons and more than fifty daughters—a vast palaceful of royal children.

Rameses had been born in the Delta. He loved its wide, wind-swept meadows, its winding waterways and its wine "sweeter than honey." So it was here, soon after he came to the throne, that Pharaoh began building his new capital, which he called Tanis. (Thebes, from this time on, became primarily a religious center.)

The new capital, like the old, was thronged with foreigners, and with natives "come to reside near the 'Sun,' " their Pharaoh. The city hummed with life and its warehouses bulged with goods from Punt, Syria, Crete, the Aegean Islands and Cyprus.

When Rameses was not in residence in his magnificent palace, which glittered with turquoise, gold and lapis lazuli, he voyaged up and down river overseeing his many building projects along the Nile. He constructed the temple of Abu Simbel above the First Cataract, with its giant statues of himself before the portals. He completed the famous Hypostyle Hall at Karnak, with its forest of pillars so big around that one hundred men could stand atop each. He built temple after temple —often with stones from the former Pharaohs' buildings,

One of Rameses' fifty daughters

Four giant statues of Rameses, each nearly seventy feet tall, guard the entrance to the temple of Abu Simbel in Upper Egypt.

which he pulled down and carted away for his own use. He even braved superstition and made off with marble and granite blocks from Akhnaton's crumbling City of the Horizon, using them to build a temple across the river.

Rameses died at the age of eighty-five, after ruling Egypt for sixty-seven long years. On the surface, the valley seemed more prosperous and stable than ever. But a closer look revealed unmistakable signs that Egypt's great days were coming to an end. The valley was in fact beginning a slow and melancholy decline into the sorry breakdown of its old age.

Egypt's decline was in part caused by a great folk-wandering that was now taking place in the ancient world. Long before Amenhotep the Third's day, tribes of land-hungry people had begun to trickle out of the vast, unknown regions north of the Black Sea. Driving their herds and flocks before them, these peoples fanned out over the ancient world. They moved down into the Tigris and Euphrates valley, and into the land that later would be called Persia. They infiltrated Asia Minor and pushed down into the mountainous peninsula of Greece. Some journeyed far overland to Italy, where they founded a little trading post on the Tiber River, which they named Rome.

History has called these peoples the Indo-Europeans. But to the ancient Egyptians they were known as the Northerners of the Islands or the Peoples of the Sea. For once they had reached the coast, many of these wanderers built themselves sleek, sharp-prowed boats and ranged the Mediterranean like hungry pirates.

During the reigns of Akhnaton and Haremhab, and of Rameses the First and Second, the trickle of wandering tribes from the north had grown into a tidal wave. The Sea Peoples crossed the Mediterranean and settled in Libya, on Egypt's western frontiers. They rolled down through Syria and Palestine, crushing the Hittites as they passed. And seventy-five years after the death of Rameses the Second they were at the very gates of Egypt herself.

Pharaoh Rameses the Third fought them off by land and sea. He kept the wanderers from invading the rich lands of the Delta. But by the end of his reign, in about 1147 B.C., the Sea Peoples had taken over Egypt's last

holdings in Palestine. The people of the Nile Valley withdrew behind their own borders. Their days as the greatest nation of the ancient world had come to an end forever.

For the next several centuries, Egypt turned this way and that, trying like a boar at bay to ward off invasion by the young and aggressive nations coming to power all about her.

But it was a losing battle. The peoples of the great folk-wandering were too many and too strong. And —more importantly—the very heart seemed to have gone out of the valley people themselves.

The Egyptians had never been a warlike people by nature. They had first gone to battle under Ahmose to rid their land of the hated Hyksos. And in an upsurge of national pride, they had willingly fought to win Thutmose the Third his empire. But then they had hired foreign mercenary, or professional, soldiers to fight their battles for them. And the valley people had turned to the comfort and security of jobs in the priesthood, or in the vast civil service that the empire demanded. During the rich and luxurious years when they controlled much of the ancient world, the Egyptians had grown so soft and complacent, so used to success and so set in their ways, that they now had neither the will to fight off the Sea Peoples, nor the flexibility to adapt themselves to the rapidly changing world around them.

Even so, the Egyptians might have enjoyed a peaceful and dignified old age in their valley—had all gone well

A few of the gigantic columns that make up the famous Hypostyle Hall at Karnak, constructed by Rameses the Second

with them there. But even nature seemed to conspire against Pharaoh's people. Not long after the death of Rameses the Third, Egypt suffered a series of disastrously low floods. Famine was severe. The starving people robbed and scavenged for food. And there was widespread dishonesty and theft among the highest government officials. It was during this time that tomb robbery became an open, and almost accepted, profession. With the connivance of guards and officials, the people systematically plundered the tombs in the Valley of the Kings, stealing the riches there to barter for food.

Strong and forceful Pharaohs might have been able to relieve Egypt's economic distress and restore order to the land. But Rameses the Third was succeeded by a long line of petty kings, one weaker than the last. Under these ineffectual rulers, the Egyptians gradually began to lose their once deep-seated faith in the divine authority of Pharaoh. He began to seem less a god to them than a weak and foolish mortal—lacking dignity, authority or strength.

Hand in hand with this loss of faith in the divinity of Pharaoh (which had been in great measure responsible for the stability and character of Egyptian society) went a growing cynicism about Egypt's great gods. The stories and songs of the period burlesque and caricature Pharaoh and the gods in a way that would have been unthinkable under Thutmose or Amenhotep or even Rameses the Second.

Thus the political and economic distress in Egypt after Rameses the Third's death was deepened by a kind of spiritual collapse among the valley people. The great days of the empire were gone. Unrest, disorder and dishonesty were rampant in the valley. And the Egyptian people had grown increasingly uncertain and cynical about the very things they had held sacred for more than two thousand years. In their troubled state, they relied ever more heavily on witchcraft, omens, demonology and oracles to solve their problems. And they shrank from the tumultuous and changing world around them. In their tired and spiritless old age, the valley people gave themselves over to dreaming of their glorious past —when, as it now seemed to them, the Egyptian world had been ordered, serene and indestructible.

Disintegration within Egypt was so rapid that some seventy-five years after the death of Rameses the Third, the valley had fallen into two separate kingdoms again. This further weakened Egypt militarily. And it was not long before the "wretched foreigner" once more ruled the land. Disordered and helpless Egypt was governed for a time by Pharaohs of Libyan descent, and then by a dynasty of invading Nubians. The downhill slide became precipitous. In 670 B.C. the bloodthirsty Assyrians overran the valley. They were followed in 525 B.C. by invading hordes of Persians. And then came young Alexander the Great. In 332 B.C. he and his world-conquering army of Macedonians and Greeks marched into Egypt, drove out the Persians and laid claim to the Nile Valley for themselves.

From time to time during the long years of foreign

occupation, a native Egyptian prince seized the throne and ruled the valley as Pharaoh for a brief time. But with the coming of Alexander the Great, Egypt's history as an independent country came to an end forever.

Alexander founded the city of Alexandria in the western Delta. And he left one of his most trusted generals, a Macedonian nobleman named Ptolemy, to govern Egypt while he marched off to win the eastern world. When Alexander died a few years later, Ptolemy seized the throne and placed the sacred Double Crown on his own head. For the next three hundred years his descendants ruled the valley as Greek Pharaohs.

And then came the turn of Rome. Queen Cleopatra, the last of the Ptolemies, committed suicide as Augustus Caesar and his formidable Roman legions marched into the Delta in 30 B.C. For the following seven hundred years Egypt served as Rome's bread basket, supplying corn to feed both the far-flung Roman legions and the citizens of the world's new capital on the Tiber River in Italy.

Then Rome's power, too, declined. In A.D. 641 the Arabs, rampaging through the Near East in the name of their prophet Mohammed, seized Egypt for themselves.

In 1517 the country was conquered once again, this time by the empire-building Turks. The Nile Valley remained under Turkish rule until young Napoleon Bonaparte and his French troops landed at Alexandria in 1798.

Almost two hundred years have passed since Napoleon and his scholars rediscovered the land of the ancient

Pharaohs. Since then, archaeologists have given the world a wondrous picture of Egypt's civilization in the great days before her decline. And, inspired by the discoveries made in the Nile Valley, other excavators have fanned out over the Near East to dig up the cities and histories of Egypt's ancient friends and enemies.

The ruins of Babylon have been found in the Tigris and Euphrates valley. In central Turkey, archaeologists have discovered the buried city of Boghaz-Köy, capital of the ancient Hittites. On Crete, the great Palace of Knossos was found beneath a hill where olive trees blew in the wind. And far to the north, the intrepid Heinrich Schliemann discovered the site of ancient Troy, where Greeks and Trojans fought their famous war during the time of Rameses the Third.

Historians often call these ancient cultures dead civilizations. But archaeologists would not agree. For there are still many gaps in their knowledge of ancient Egypt and her world. And there are still many known areas to be excavated in Egypt and the Near East—to say nothing of unknown sites still to be discovered, and of the exciting accidental finds of archaeology.

In 1954, for example, a group of Arab workmen were building a new tourist road around the Great Pyramid of Giza. Not twenty-five yards from the base of the pyramid, and in ground archaeologists thought held no more secrets for them, the workmen uncovered a line of huge stone blocks. Beneath them lay a full-sized wooden ship. It had been buried with Pharaoh Cheops five thousand years earlier, so that his spirit could sail up and down the Nile after death, as the Pharaoh had done during his lifetime.

And so, until every possible scrap of evidence has been found and evaluated, the civilizations of Egypt and the ancient Near East are very much alive to archaeologists. Their exciting and painstaking work continues. And scarcely a month goes by that the newspapers of the world do not report a new find, large or small, somewhere in the Nile Valley or in the ancient lands that bounded its world.

Photograph Credits

Alfred Wagg from Alpha Associates, pages 56–57, 112; Alpha Associates, Inc., page 15; Black Star, pages 155, 163; The British Museum, pages 7, 53, 68, 122; The Brooklyn Museum, pages 28 (right), 50 (top), 124; Egyptian State Tourist Administration, page 43; Griffith Institute, page 148; The Metropolitan Museum of Art, pages ii, 60 (lower left and right), 72, 89, 99, 103, 116, 136, 142, 166; The Metropolitan Museum of Art, Harry Burton, page 144; The Metropolitan Museum of Art, Dodge Fund 1931, page 31; The Metropolitan Museum of Art, Gift of Edward S. Harkness 1925, page 50 (middle); The Metropolitan Museum of Art, Egyptian Expedition, pages 46, 82, 108; The Metropolitan Museum of Art, Rogers Fund 1907, page 66; Rogers Fund 1912, page 28 (upper left); Rogers Fund 1926, page 50 (bottom); Pat Morin from Monkmeyer, page 23; Monkmeyer, page 164; Museum of Fine Arts, Boston, pages 28 (lower left), 60 (top); George Holton from Photo Researchers, pages 33, 41, 77, 94, 133, 161; Lawrence Smith from Photo Researchers, page 85; Royal Scottish Museum, page vii; Wide World Photos, pages 11, 151.

The quotation on pages 149–150 is reprinted by permission of Cooper Square Publishers, Inc., from *The Tomb of Tutankhamen* by Howard Carter and A. C. Mace (Cooper Square Publishers, 1963), volume I, pages 95–100.

Index

References to photographs are in *italic type*.

Relive history!

Turn the page for more great books . . .

Landmark Books® Grades 6 and Up

Landmark Books® Grades 4 and Up

Landmark Books® Grades 2 and Up